# THE FIRST CHRISTIAN DRAMA

## BOOKS BY JOHN WICK BOWMAN

*Published by The Westminster Press*

THE FIRST CHRISTIAN DRAMA:
 The Book of Revelation
(*originally*, THE DRAMA OF THE BOOK OF REVELATION)

PROPHETIC REALISM AND THE GOSPEL

THE INTENTION OF JESUS

# THE FIRST CHRISTIAN DRAMA

## THE BOOK OF REVELATION

by

JOHN WICK BOWMAN

**THE WESTMINSTER PRESS**

PHILADELPHIA

Library of Congress Catalog Card No. 68–19049

Published by The Westminster Press®
Philadelphia, Pennsylvania

PRINTED IN THE UNITED STATES OF AMERICA

*To*

J.S.B. — M.B.W. — D.C.B.
N.J.B. — J.C.W. — B.C.B.

*as well as to the younger generation*
a rich treasury of personalities

> The victor I shall make a pillar
> in the sanctuary of my God —
> he will never leave it.
> *Revelation 3:12*

# Preface

THIS little volume represents an endeavor to provide a wholesome guidebook to the most abused writing in the Christian Scriptures. In general, treatises on The Revelation to John written at the level of the intelligent layman have issued from the pens of those who either mistake the author's original intent in writing or else exhibit no concern to discover it. Whatever be the faults attaching to the present attempt — and no doubt they are many — at any rate it may not be said in fairness that the writer has not striven to understand the prophet, John.

My conviction is that the key to such understanding is to be discovered in the structure of the book. As will appear, it is treated here as a " drama " upon whose literary form is superimposed, no doubt by the original author himself, another — that of a letter, with a view to its securing the attention of the whole Church for which its message was intended. To dispose of this superimposed letter form is a matter of a few moments' observation. This is done in the Introduction, which follows. What remains occupies our attention throughout the rest of the book. It is a drama quite artificially constructed of seven acts in each of which occur seven scenes.

The artificiality of this literary structure gives evidence of a nicely conceived plan on the author's part to present his living message in a telling way. His theme is the " Christian Theology of History," or an account of the working out of the gospel on the plane of temporal human affairs and its consummation in the salvation of the Church.

7

This is not to say that John did not *see* his "visions," nor is it to deny the presence of revelation in the book. John was a prophet of God — of this there can be no doubt. It is, indeed, because his book is replete with the prophetic message and spirit that it is included within the pages of Scripture, while numerous other apocalyptic writings lacking that message and spirit have been excluded. The Church under the guidance of the Spirit chose wisely here.

But, whereas most of us think in abstract terms, John thought in pictures or concrete images. Revelation came to him, accordingly, in the form he could understand and assimilate. Whatever be the nature of our thought processes, however, we shall find here a presentation of the gospel message that is as mentally stimulating as it is heart-warming. The artificial character of the book's structure — the creation of an undoubted literary artist — greatly enhances the interest of its content, even as the imagery present to its author's mind — however foreign this may seem to our ways of thinking — contributes a certain fascination to the ideas with which he deals.

No attempt has been made to give credit to the numerous books that have aided my own thought about John's Revelation. This single expression of my indebtedness to their authors must be allowed to afford sufficient payment of the great debt I owe them. The translation — better perhaps, the paraphrase — is my own: in general it follows Nestle's well-known Greek text (the twenty-first edition). I have not hesitated, however, at numerous points to adopt a wording that departs from this text and in my judgment better represents the prophet's mind. Though generally endeavoring to make the book speak the language of today, I have at times indulged in archaisms because such appeared to suit the prophetic nature of the message.

# Introduction

J OHN'S BOOK is unique among "apocalypses" in having the form of both a letter and a drama. All such literature is dramatic in style. This is true of pagan apocalypses like Virgil's *Aeneid,* as well as of the later Christian examples of which Dante's *Inferno* and Milton's *Paradise Lost* are typical. The same may be said of those like I Enoch, The Apocalypse of Baruch, and IV Esdras, which are popularly known as "apocrypha."

John's apocalypse alone is also a letter. It opens and closes like any other communication of the day. This complicates the problem of understanding it. It also enhances its value. For John knows himself in possession of a message urgently needed by the Church. It is to stress this urgency that he gives his book the intimate, personally oriented form of a common letter.

## a. *John's Title for His Book*

Naturally, since John's apocalypse is a book in the dramatic style it has a title. This is found in the first three verses of the first chapter. Originally these verses were probably written on a label attached to the outside of the book. This title reads —

## THE APOCALYPSE OF JESUS CHRIST

— which God allowed him to dramatize for the benefit of his followers — being a revelation of events speedily impending. Sending by his messenger, he delivered it in code to John (a mere slave of his); accordingly, the things within, of which he remarks that he "saw" them, repre-

9

sent his endeavor to testify to this Word of God, or rather to Jesus Christ's dramatic statement of it.

Blessings on the official " reader " of the words of this prophetic message, on the listening congregation, and particularly on those who observe to live in accord with what is written in it — for the appointed occasion to which it refers is near. (1:1-3)

In ancient times books were written on sheets of parchment or papyrus, which were sewed together at the sides. The whole collection was rolled up in the form of a scroll. About A.D. 150 or a little earlier the book form (called codex) with which we are familiar made its first appearance. At that time the title, which as above stated had previously been attached to the outside, was transferred to the inside " title page." This, it seems, is what happened to the first three verses of John's Revelation.

What is meant by the term " apocalypse " which John employs in his title? To begin with, it is the Greek word meaning " a revelation." It is applied to the dramatic literature that flourished among both Jews and Christians between 175 B.C. and A.D. 100. In some cases writers of both faiths worked over or edited and reedited the same books. They represent an earnest attempt on the part of their authors to write a philosophy or theology of history. That is to say, they endeavor to furnish the answers to vital questions such as these: Has history a meaning? a purpose? a goal? Is it " getting anywhere "? Will good or evil eventually triumph? And in either case, why and how? Is God's hand discernible in the affairs of men? Is he actually directing the course of events? Is it perchance his purpose that history fulfills in the end?

John claims that his apocalypse was sponsored by God himself, delivered by him to Jesus, and transmitted by the latter to the author through *his messenger* (Gk. angel). Angels generally have served as the means of communication in this type of literature. John is here merely following the usual pattern. Like a wise teacher he adopts the modes of expression, the terminology, even the thought frames to which his readers are accustomed. He claims later, however, to have direct contact with Jesus Christ (vs. 12 ff.) — the angel, accordingly, is scarcely more than a literary device with him.

John earnestly hopes that the Church will read, assimilate, and *live in accord with* the teaching of the book. The note of urgency in his writing is unmistakable: undoubtedly it is the work of one endowed with the true pastoral instinct — that of the " good shepherd " ever mindful of the saving of his flock. It is also far closer to the *prophetic message* and to the writings of the Hebrew prophets in both spirit and content than any other of the apocalypses known to us. These latter appear, indeed, quite openly to ignore the prophets, whereas John quotes them verbatim in almost 150 separate passages! Little wonder that he should consider himself also to rank among the prophets and his writing as prophecy (22:7, 10, 18 f.). Like those older prophets, therefore, John thinks of himself as the recipient of a revelation charged with the very *Word of God* itself (1:2, 9; 3:8, 10; 6:9; 12:11; 19:13; 20:4).

### b. The Letter Form of This Apocalypse

As already remarked, John's apocalypse assumes the form of both a letter and a drama. This dual form imparts to it a somewhat complicated appearance. But we shall experience little difficulty on this account if we but note that the letter form appears only in the Opening Salutation (1:4–6) and in the Closing Benediction (22:21). All that lies between is drama. As a letter, then, John's apocalypse possesses an Opening Salutation, reading —

John
To the Seven Churches in Asia!

Grace and peace to you — from the One who is and was and is coming — from the seven spirits before his throne — from Jesus Christ, the faithful witness, the first-born from among the dead, the Ruler of the kings of earth.

To him who loves us and who has loosed us from our sins by his blood — he has formed of us a Kingdom; he has appointed us priests toward God, even his Father — to him be glory and might into eternity. Amen. (1:4-6)

John's opening salutation contains the three parts characteristic of all Christian letters of the period — " salutation proper " (" *John, to the seven churches in Asia* "), " blessing " (" *Grace and peace . . . earth* "), and " doxology " or prayer (" *To him who loves. . . . Amen* "). It was probably Paul who first adopted the practice of combining the Hebrew and Greek modes of salutation as represented by the words " grace " and " peace " at the opening of his letters (see I Thess. 1:1 for his simplest style). " Grace " in the Greek is *charis,* the noun meaning " love functioning under adverse conditions " and deriving from the same stem as the Greek *chairein* (" cheer up ") generally employed as a form of salutation among Greeks. " Grace," then, is " cheer up " baptized by the Christian gospel and suggestive of a valid reason for doing so to be found in God's love which operates in spite of the adverse circumstance created by man's rebellion against His will. " Peace," again, is the usual Semitic mode of salutation (*shālōm, salaam*), equivalent of the medieval monk's *pax tecum.* But once again it becomes in Biblical circles a " peace " emanating from God himself and directed with saving intent toward man. In the Hebrew it often stands for " salvation."

The *Asia* mentioned in the salutation is the Roman province that went by that name, not the continent nor even Asia Minor as we use the term. Note that in giving expression to the ideas set forth here, John uses a sort of pre-trinitarian formula to describe the nature of God (" *The One who is . . . the seven spirits . . . Jesus Christ* "). It was out of the wish to give expression to the experience of God lying behind such terms that the Church of the fourth century developed its doctrine of the Trinity.

The doxology contains several elements which are to find later development in the drama — *loosed us, his blood, formed of us a Kingdom, appointed us priests*. This is the language of the tabernacle, the temple, and sacrifice — the teaching of this book throughout is presented against a background formed by these paraphernalia of worship.

John's letter closes with a Benediction, which runs —

> The grace of the Lord Jesus
> Be with you all,
> Even with you — his saints.
> Amen.
>
> (22:21)

### c. John's Seven-Act Drama

John's drama, like the Graeco-Latin drama of his day, includes a Prologue (1:7, 8) and an Epilogue (22:6-20) discussed at the appropriate points (pp. 19 and 157–159).

Between these two features of the drama, there lie seven *acts* (usually termed " visions "). Four of these acts are characterized by *stage props* taken from the furnishings of tabernacle and temple (p. 25), together with sevenfold divisions termed " letters," " seals," " trumpets," and " bowls," which in a drama correspond to *scenes*. On these points all commentators are fairly agreed.

It remains, then, merely to demonstrate that a similar format is found as well in the three remaining acts. That this is so is clear as regards the *stage props* (pp. 76, 110, and 140). But John changed his method of indicating a change of scenes for these three acts. Instead of distinguishing these as above described, he has employed the Greek verbs meaning " I saw " (*eidon*), " there appeared " (*ōphthē*), or " I shall show *you* " (*deixō soi*) and " he showed *me* " (*edeixen moi*) for this purpose.

With a view to indicating such change of stage props and scenes for three acts, obviously one or other of these verbs would require to be used three times for the stage props and twenty-one times for the scenes, or twenty-four times in all. Actually,

13

the four verbs in question occur twenty-seven times in this part of the drama, as follows: " I saw " (*eidon*) — twenty times, at 13:1, 2, 11; 14:1, 6, 14; 15:2; 17:3, 6; 18:1; 19:11, 17, 19; 20:1, 4, 11, 12; 21:1, 2, 22; " there appeared " (*ōphthē*) — three times, at 11:19; 12:1, 3; "I shall show you" (*deixō soi*) — twice, at 17:1; 21:9; and " he showed me " (*edeixen moi*) — twice, at 21:10; 22:1.

The difference between the twenty-four and twenty-seven occurrences of these four verbs is due to duplications at 12:1, 3 (p. 78); 13:1, 2 (p. 84); and 21:9, 10 (p. 150).

A check on the accuracy of these divisions is provided by the fact that, just as Acts III and V are co-ordinates, each covering the same materials from two different viewpoints (see comments on p. 63 and pp. 99 to 107), so there is a clear co-ordination between Acts IV and VI. A discussion of this co-ordination will be found on pp. 111 to 135. This co-ordination includes, for example, the two women at 12:1 ff. and 17:3 ff.; the two Beasts at 13:1 ff. and 17:6 ff.; the second Beast at 13:11 ff. and the celebration of its destruction at 18:1 to 19:10; the Lamb and its retinue with the Word of God and his followers at 14:1-5 and 19:11 ff.; the angels at 14:6 ff. and 19:17 f., and the like. No such check may be applied to Act VII, but the divisions into stage setting and scenes follow the usage of the verbs mentioned.

Who, then, was this John, the Seer? We do not know, nor is the answer of any great significance. It should suffice that he was one truly inspired by the Spirit of the living God to write a message fraught with large import for the progress of the gospel. Those who must know the identity of an artist in order to evaluate a painting do not appreciate art! So of divine revelation — either it is self-authenticating, or else it is not divine revelation. No matter who its author be, this book breathes the Spirit of the Lord of Life.

John's drama breathes its author's strong faith in the Church's triumphant march to victory and in God's eventual fulfillment of his saving purpose relative to mankind.

# Contents

# PROLOGUE

## PROLOGUE

*A herald announces —*

"Behold! He comes with the clouds!
Every eye will behold him, even those who impaled him.
All earth's tribes will be grievously 'cut up' over him.
Yea. Amen."

The Lord God says, "I am the 'Alpha' and the 'Omega,' the One who is and who was and who comes, the Almighty."

(1:7, 8)

THE DRAMA opens with the shouts of two figures! The curtain is not yet drawn back. We have seen none of the stage props, nor have we been introduced to the setting for the action. Two prophetic characters emerge from behind the curtain, so to speak, and cry their parts. One is a herald; the other is the Lord God himself.

The effect is rather startling. For this is a cosmic stage and the action is to have cosmic significance. That herald is announcing the motif of the play — *History's most notable Person is about to appear again on history's stage.* He came before " unheralded and unsung." It will not be so a second time. Before he was " despised and rejected " — his rejecters will now have food for thought! For all will see him, and his rank will now be clear above peradventure of doubt.

Lest there be doubt, the Lord God speaks. We should expect God to refer to himself as " the One who is and who was and who *is to be.*" But for the last of these three clauses he substitutes *who comes,* thus identifying himself with the coming One announced by the herald! Could anything better enhance our anticipation of this drama's significance?

The Prologue — with its narrators (often one of the Greek pantheon) who introduced the play — was a creation of the Attic stage. It was further developed long before John's day by Latins like Plautus. Aeschylus' *Agamemnon* even opens with a soliloquy of a "watchman." But the watchman or herald of " good tidings, who publishes peace, . . . who says to Zion, ' Your God reigns,' " in Second Isaiah is nearer to John's spirit and theme (Isa. 52:7 ff.). Then too, the latter's herald quotes in large part from Dan. 7:13 and Zech. 12:10 ff. So, while John's drama wears a Greek dress, it proclaims a message in the best Hebrew prophetic-Christian tradition.

# Act

# I

# VISION OF THE CHURCH ON EARTH

## *The Son of Man in Its Midst*

(Chs. 1:9 to 3:22)

*Stage Setting:* The Seven Golden Lampstands (1:9–20)

### THE LETTERS TO THE SEVEN CHURCHES (2:1 to 3:22)

Scene 1   Letter to the Passionless Church: Ephesus (2:1–7)

Scene 2   Letter to the Persecuted Church: Smyrna (2:8–11)

Scene 3   Letter to the Tolerant Church: Pergamum (2:12–17)

Scene 4   Letter to the Compromising Church: Thyatira (2:18–29)

Scene 5   Letter to the Dead Church: Sardis (3:1–6)

Scene 6   Letter to the Missionary Church: Philadelphia (3:7–13)

Scene 7   Letter to the Arrogant Church: Laodicea (3:14–22)

*Stage Setting: The Seven Golden Lampstands* (*1:9–20*)

(As the curtain is drawn back on this cosmic stage, we see upon it two figures only — a *narrator*, John, the Seer; and the *Son of Man*. The center of the stage is occupied by seven lampstands of gold arranged in the form of a circle or alternatively of a seven-branched candelabra, as explained below.)

*The narrator speaks* —

I, John, your brother and comrade in the tribulation, sovereignty, and endurance which we share in Jesus, "chanced upon" the island called Patmos — this was because I had declared God's Word and testified to Jesus.

Accordingly, on the Lord's Day I came deeply under the Spirit's influence and heard behind me a loud voice not unlike the shrill notes of a trumpet. It addressed me thus:

"Write down in a book what you are about to see and send it to the seven churches — to Ephesus, to Smyrna, to Pergamum, to Thyatira, to Sardis, to Philadelphia, and to Laodicea."

(1:9–11)

JOHN ACTS as narrator — a functionary the like of which accompanies various types of dramatic art. As such, like the Hebrew prophets, he directs our thoughts toward the theology of history which is the theme of the drama's teaching. He is also to be identified with Bunyan's Evangelist, for the content of his drama is the gospel message. " Prophecy," " theology of history," " gospel ": such great words define for us the subject of this book. Through it all and in the midst of its strenuous activities, we are never permitted to lose sight of the narrator who is the witness to these themes. Always John is that little figure at the side of the stage of God's activity — observing keenly, reporting faithfully what he sees.

John's *" chanced upon "* . . . *Patmos* is a euphemism for banishment to the marble quarries for which under the Roman emperors this penal colony was infamous. This is the first mention in Christian literature of the *Lord's Day,* stressing as it does the fact of our Lord's resurrection on Sunday. Possibly, however, John is using the phrase in the sense of Amos 5:18 — that is, of the " lost times " in which John thinks himself as writing. (See also Heb. 1:12; I John 2:18.)

A glance at the map of the Roman province of Asia shows the *seven churches* to be arranged in the form of the seven-branched candlestick of the Herodian Temple — Nos. 1 and 7, 2 and 6, 3 and 5 forming pairs on opposite sides with No. 4 at the top. This is significant as we shall later have occasion to observe. John, however, speaks of them as lampstands for purposes of his stage setting and that the " Son of Man " may be seen walking in their midst (v. 13; 2:1).

*Stage Setting* (Continued)

### THE "SON OF MAN" AND THE SEVEN LAMPSTANDS OF GOLD

I looked round to discover the owner of the voice speaking to me. As I turned, I beheld seven lampstands of gold and, in the midst of these lampstands, as it were a "Son of Man." He was garbed in a loose robe reaching to the feet, about which was wound at the chest level a strand of gold. His head and hair were as white as wool or as snow; his eyes were like a fiery flame for brilliance; his feet shone as any brasslike metal shines while being heated in a furnace; his voice was as the sound of a great rush of water. He held in his right hand seven stars. From out of his mouth there proceeded a sharp, double-edged sword. His countenance was as brilliant as the sun at full strength.

When I saw him, I fell at his feet as though dead.

But he placed his right hand on me and said: "Do not fear. I am the First and the Last and the Living One. I suffered death — but lo! I live into eternity. I possess, moreover, the keys of death and the grave. Then write about what you see — about contemporary events and about those destined to transpire hereafter. As for the secret of the seven stars which you see in my right hand and of the seven lampstands of gold — the seven stars are the spiritually mature of the seven churches, while the seven lampstands are the seven churches." (1:12–20)

J OHN *looked round* to see who spoke with him, and his eyes fell upon the *seven churches!* This was right and proper, seeing that the speaker was about to be revealed as Jesus Christ. The Church is precisely the spot where he is to be found in the world. It has been said that Church history is an extension of the biography of Jesus — that biography has never yet been written for the reason that it is incomplete to date. Jesus Christ still lives — he is alive in the Church, which is his " body." Would one " see Jesus "? Then let him turn his eyes toward the historic Church, for it is here that he is to be found — such is the profound message of this passage.

" *Son of Man* " was the term by which Jesus referred to himself, as all the Gospels testify. It is the risen, glorified Christ who is seen and described by John. The Semitic imagery which meets us in this apocalypse is not meant to be visualized, nor to be reproduced in art. It is intended rather to convey a message. It is symbolical, presenting the outer symbol of the inner, spiritual reality. The picture of the eternal Christ which meets us here is no exception — he is described in terms of royalty and divinity taken largely from Dan. 7:13; 10:6 f. and Ezek. 9:2 ff.

The stage props for every act in this drama are adapted from the tabernacle and temple. Here the seven-branched candelabra of the sanctuary is employed, and most appropriately as the Church considered itself both sanctuary or dwelling place of God on earth (Eph. 2:19–22) and the world's light (Matt. 5:14–16). *Seven,* as always among Semites, stands for completeness — hence, *seven churches* signifies the Church Universal.

## LETTER TO THE PASSIONLESS CHURCH: *Ephesus*

*Write this —*

To the Spiritually Mature of the Church at Ephesus —

He who keeps the seven stars safe in his right hand, who walks in the midst of the seven golden lampstands, says:

" I am cognizant of your works — your labor, your steadfastness; that you are unable to abide evildoers; that you have tested those who acclaim themselves apostles though they are not and that you have adjudged them liars; that you are showing endurance and bearing up for my name's sake without weariness.

" But I have this against you — you have left off your initial love.

" Remember, then, how far you have fallen away. Repent. Do again those first works. If not, I shall come to you. I shall remove your lampstand from its allotted place, if you do not repent. But you do have this much — you hate the deeds of the Nicolaitans. I hate them too.

" Whoever has an ear, let him hearken to what the Spirit says to the churches.

" To the victor, I shall grant that he may eat of the Tree of Life that is found in God's Paradise." (2:1–7)

ACT I portrays the spiritual condition of the Church in the world. Throughout it but two characters appear — the "Son of Man" is seen dictating to the seer, his amanuensis.

In this first scene the eternal Christ is depicted in terms of his most vital relations with his Church. As he *keeps* it in the palm of *his right hand,* he is its Redeemer — as he *walks in the midst* of his Church on earth, he is its Lord.

The Lord Jesus has the most intimate knowledge of the condition of his Church. Nothing is hid from his eyes. He has seen that the Ephesian church is capable of discerning who are false *apostles* — these possibly are legalistic Christians attempting to bind the Church with " do's and don't's." Their opposite number are the *Nicolaitans* — probably a group who in the name of "freedom" are carrying on a life of licentiousness. Their leader may have been the Nicolaus of Acts 6:5. *The Church at Ephesus* has escaped these two extremes of legalism and corrupt living.

But this church has left off its *initial love.* It is resting on its past laurels and traditions. The element of surprise, of creativity, is lacking in its life. There are no heresies here — but there is also no life, no warmth, no real love.

Will Christ commend such a church? He will not. In effect he says: "You *hate* some things, do you? — so do I. But there is no creativity in hate. Only love can bring forth life. *Repent,* then, and relearn the art of loving."

But to those spirits in whom there is still love and life because they are really *victors,* he promises the *Tree of Life* throughout eternity!

## LETTER TO THE PERSECUTED CHURCH: *Smyrna*

*Write this —*

To the Spiritually Mature of the Church at Smyrna —

The First and the Last who suffered death and has come alive says:

" I am aware of your tribulation and poverty — you are really rich though — and of the blasphemous talk of those who call themselves Jews though they are not. Satan's synagogue is what they are!

" Do not be fearful of what you are about to suffer. Lo! the Devil is on the point of casting some of you into prison for your testing. You will have a short period of trial — say, ten days. Go on being faithful — even unto death. I shall give you the Crown of Life.

" Whoever has an ear, let him hearken to what the Spirit says to the churches.

" The victor will never be hurt by the second death." (2:8–11)

S MYRNA is the typical martyr church. Everything here suggests this. The speaker describes himself in terms of *death* and resurrection — the body of the letter speaks of *trial* and *testing* — the promise held out to the church is the *Crown* which is *Life* indeed — the prize of the *victor* is that he will escape the *second death*. No letter in the series exhibits more literary unity.

The persecutors here are doubtless the local Jewish community. They pride themselves on their blood, but they are not the real *Jews,* as Paul has pointed out (Rom. 2:28 f.). The true Israel is composed of those who acknowledge Jesus Christ (I Peter 2:1-10). By rejecting him the old Jewish people have given up their right to be called God's people — rather they are a veritable *Satan's synagogue* (John 8:39 ff.).

*Ten days* — what a trivial amount of time compared with the eternity of God's blessings awaiting the martyrs! The *second death* is equated with being cast into *the lake that burns with fire and brimstone* (21:8) — a figurative expression meaning banishment forever from God's fellowship, as the context there shows. Christians are not promised that they will escape the sufferings and final physical death shared by all men. God cares for his people by granting them a spirit of fortitude and hope such as the world cannot know.

Only the persecuted and missionary churches — Smyrna and Philadelphia — escape some warning of punishment for their sins. Too, the letters addressed to them contain no call to repentance. These churches, by reason of their witness-bearing even unto death, are fulfilling their Lord's will. He desires nothing of his Church save that it remain *faithful* to its trust, the gospel.

## LETTER TO THE TOLERANT CHURCH: *Pergamum*

*Write this —*

To the Spiritually Mature of the Church at Pergamum —

He who has the sharp, double-edged sword, says:

"I know where you live — at Satan's capital! You are holding onto my name. You did not deny your faith in me even in the days of Antipas, my witness, my faithful one, who was liquidated in your midst — that's where Satan lives!

"But I do have several things against you. You have there a number that hold the teaching of Balaam who taught Balak to put a stumbling block in the way of the sons of Israel — the eating of food dedicated at a pagan shrine and fornication. You have some who accept the teaching of the Nicolaitans which is of like nature.

"Now then, repent. Otherwise I intend to come to you speedily and make war on such with the sword in my mouth.

"Whoever has an ear, let him hearken to what the Spirit says to the churches.

"To the victor I shall give some of the hidden Manna. I shall give him too a white ballot, and upon the ballot a new name inscribed, which no one knows except the recipient." (2:12–17)

THIS CHURCH and the two that follow form a trio. They represent respectively courtship, seduction, and death at Satan's hands. At Pergamum the Church is seen in courtship's indecisive frenzy! The evil suitor is being tolerated. True — this " Vanity Fair " is no saints' rest for those who would follow the Christian way. It is the center of the imperial cult for the province and so *Satan's capital!* This worship of the State in the emperor's person enjoys the prestige attaching to secular power.

There were those in the church at Pergamum — *Nicolaitans* with perhaps a self-styled " prophet " like *Balaam* at their head — who argued that food dedicated at the imperial shrine and then sold in the markets had not been contaminated for Christian use. Even Paul had agreed that " an idol has no real existence " (I Cor. 8:4), and it could be argued that what has no existence cannot alter food offered to it.

But this amounted to flirtation with the pagan deity and disloyalty to the only true God. Such toleration could not be countenanced within the Christian Church. Paul had also said: " What pagans sacrifice, they offer to demigods, not to God. . . . You cannot, then, partake of the Table of the Lord and the table of these demigods at the same time " (I Cor. 10:20 f.). The church must *repent* of its laxity, else *the double-edged sword* of the gospel would deal out, not salvation, but damnation to it.

The *victor* is to receive a *white ballot* secretly *inscribed* with the *new name* of his Redeemer in token of intimate knowledge and understanding. He is also to eat of God's *hidden Manna* — the spiritual banquet long promised to God's people to replace the idolatrous feast!

## LETTER TO THE COMPROMISING CHURCH: *Thyatira*

*Write this —*

To the Spiritually Mature of the Church at Thyatira —

Thus says the Son of God, who has eyes like fiery flames and feet like brass cast in a furnace:

" I am acquainted with your works — with your love and faith, your service and perseverance. I know too that your recent deeds are more conspicuously praiseworthy than those of a former time.

" But I hold this against you — you put up with that woman, Jezebel, who calls herself a prophetess. Her teaching and cunning have led astray my servants into adultery and the eating of idolatrous sacrificial food.

" I have given her a reasonable time to repent of her thoroughly evil ways, but she will not do it. Lo! I intend to make her a present of a bed on which to lie — one of great torment — it will be for her ' lovers ' as well unless they turn from her type of deed. As for her spawn — I shall finish them off with death. Then, all the churches will recognize that it is I who really am cognizant of man's motivations and affections, and that I intend to requite to each according to his works.

" To the rest of you in Thyatira who do not hold with this teaching — to you who have not acquainted yourselves with ' Satan's profundities,' as they call them — I have only this to say, ' I have no other load to put upon your shoulders than this: until I come, hold onto what you have! ' To the victor who keeps at the sort of work I desire to the finish I shall give authority over the nations — ' he shall shepherd them with an iron rod; he shall crush them as though they were vessels of pottery.' I shall present him also with the Morning Star which I had from my Father.

" Whoever has an ear, let him hearken to what the Spirit says to the churches." (2:18–29)

THE CHURCH at Thyatira has gone farther down the hill of destruction than that at Pergamum. Satan's courtship of it has advanced to the point of actual seduction. The leader of the evil forces in this church is a woman and she has numerous " *lovers*." The sin which she sponsors is for this drama of the very essence of evil — it is adherence to a religion of the State as promoted by a pagan culture — it is the exalting of the trappings of a secular civilization till these become rivals of God himself for man's loyalty, reverence, and love.

*Satan's profundities* here sounds like an intentioned opposite to Paul's " God's profundities " (I Cor. 2:10). The popular religions of the day all stressed their secrets — known only to the initiate into these " mysteries." It would be a bold *prophetess*, indeed, who would advertise her wares as the mysteries of Satan! And yet the history of the Church has seen others of her ilk. The so-called " holy devil," Rasputin, the renegade monk at the court of the last of the czars, appears to have taught that to be forgiven any particular sin, one must first be initiated into its secret, commit it, then seek forgiveness for it! A Devil's *badspel*, indeed.

The *Son of God* will not tolerate such teaching and acting in his Church. His *eyes* burn with *fiery flames* against those who dare so to contaminate his holy people — his *feet* will tread them in judgment.

To the *victor* who resists this evil influence, the Church's Lord will reserve a unique sort of *authority over the nations* — a moral force which will sway them as *with an iron rod*. This force is like the *Morning Star* in its promise of a new day in which righteousness only will be found.

## LETTER TO THE DEAD CHURCH: *Sardis*

*Write this —*

To the Spiritually Mature of the Church at Sardis —

He who possesses the seven spirits of God and the seven stars says:

" I have uncovered your works — you have a reputation for being alive but you are really dead. Wake up — try to give some sort of support to the part of you that is not yet quite dead!

" For I have not found any of your deeds that could be labeled 'a finished product' in the sight of God.

" Recall, then, how you received the Christian tradition, how you heard the gospel. Keep it safe and repent. If you do not wake up, I shall come like a thief — nor will you ever know at what hour I propose to come upon you.

" However, you do have a few persons in Sardis who have not soiled their clothing. They will walk with me in white, for they are worthy. The victor will be dressed in white garments after the same fashion. Nor shall I ever blot his name out of the Book of Life — rather I shall acknowledge his name in the presence of my Father and of his angels.

" Whoever has an ear, let him hearken to what the Spirit says to the churches." (3:1–6)

W HAT A SAD COMMENT on a church's life — *a reputation* and no character to back it up! Like Marley, this church was *dead* — " of that there could be no doubt." But Marley's ghost had *a reputation for being alive* and so have a thousand nominal churches. Yet a " dead church " is a contradiction in terms. For *Spirit* and *Star* (i.e., Church) go together, and where the Spirit is there must be life. " The discipline whereby the Spirit produces life in Christ Jesus liberates from a discipline that brings forth only sin and death " (Rom. 8:2). Where there is death, then, the Spirit is not present and the Church is nonexistent.

But there was a *part* even of this church at Sardis that was *not yet quite dead*. " Hope springs eternal " in the breast of the Church's Lord. He will not desert even this corpse for the sake of the *few persons . . . who have not soiled their clothing*. We are reminded of God's gracious attitude toward Sodom and Gomorrah (Gen. 18:33) — " for the sake of ten " persons he would not destroy these wicked cities.

The one treasure any church ever has that is worth preserving to the end is what it has *received* as a link in the sacred chain of *tradition* stretching back to the earliest days of the Church's life. This is the *gospel* message committed to its trust. At times in this book one hears echoes of the Master's very words spoken while he walked among men and treasured up in the Church's storehouse of memories. In this letter these echoes appear to be particularly numerous — *I shall come like a thief* (see Luke 12:39) — the *hour* of his coming (Mark 13:32) — the *name* written down in heaven (Luke 10:20) — confession *in the presence of my Father* (Matt. 10:32), *and of his angels* (Luke 12:9). These memories preserved in John's mind link the eternal Spirit unmistakably with the historic Jesus of Nazareth.

SCENE 6

## LETTER TO THE MISSIONARY CHURCH: *Philadelphia*

*Write this —*

To the Spiritually Mature of the Church at Philadelphia —
So speaks the holy and faithful One, who possesses the key of David, who opens and none may close, who closes and none may open:

" I am mindful of your works — lo! I have placed before you an open door such as no one can close. For you possess some little power — you have kept my Word safe and have not denied my name.

" Look — I am going to assign to your care some of ' Satan's synagogue ' who call themselves Jews though they are not — liars is what they are! Lo! I shall have them come and do obeisance at your feet — so shall they learn how much I have loved you. As you have kept my counsel to endure, so I shall shield you from the hour of testing which is about to come upon mankind with a view to trying out earth's inhabitants.

" I am coming quickly. Hold fast to what you have lest someone take away your crown. The victor I shall make a pillar in the sanctuary of my God — he will never leave it. Moreover, I shall inscribe on his countenance the name of my God, the name of my God's City — New Jerusalem, the City that is about to come down out of heaven from my God — and my own new name.

" Whoever has an ear to hear, let him hearken to what the Spirit says to the churches." (3:7-13)

36

THERE IS an unmistakable parallelism between the letter to this church and the one to the church at Smyrna. Both are witnessing churches — both are in contact with those *who call themselves Jews* (Jews by birth, not by rebirth) — both are to receive *the Crown of Life*. The difference is largely one of stress. As regards Smyrna tribulation to be endured receives the main emphasis, in the case of Philadelphia, opportunity for witness-bearing and service in the eternal *sanctuary*.

The description of the letter's author here is taken almost verbatim from Isa. 22:22 — there the future high priest of Judah is portrayed; here, the eternal High Priest who *possesses* the *key* with which to *open* the *door* into the circle of God's people, the house of *David*.

What a rich reward is in prospect for the faithful here! It consists in greater opportunity for service — such a one becomes an eternal *pillar in the sanctuary* of God, supporting in heaven as on earth the meeting place between God and man. On earth these faithful had been " the pillars of the Church " — their reward is to continue to occupy this place of distinction and service in the eternities ahead. It is upon such pillars of the heavenly temple also that those who tread its halls will find suitably *inscribed* the *name* of God, that of *God's City,* and the *new name* of the City's redeemer — a finely picturesque way of saying that witnessing Christians through living fellowship with God come to bear the imprint of his nature. It is they who fulfill God's original design that man shall reflect his image and share his likeness (Gen. 1:26).

# LETTER TO THE ARROGANT CHURCH: *Laodicea*

*Write this —*

To the Spiritually Mature of the Church at Laodicea —

Thus says the Amen, the faithful and true Witness, the Beginning of God's creation:

"I have come to know of your works — you are neither cold nor hot. I could wish that you were either cold or hot. So, since you are lukewarm and neither hot nor cold, I propose to spew you out of my mouth!

"You say: 'I am rich. I have become wealthy. I have no need of anything.' What you do not know is that you are poverty-stricken, pitiable, beggarly, blind, naked. Let me counsel you to buy of me gold purified by fire if you really want riches, white garments if you would be clothed in reality and the shame of your nakedness is not to be exposed, eye salve to anoint your eyes if you care about true insight.

"Whom I love, I test and chastise. Show some interest, then, and repent.

"Look — I am standing at the door and knocking. If anyone listens to my voice and opens the door, I shall come in and dine with him and he with me. To the victor I shall grant to sit beside me on my throne, just as when victorious I sat down with my Father on his throne.

"Whoever has an ear to hear, let him hearken to what the Spirit says to the churches." (3:14–22)

T HIS LAODICEAN CHURCH is similar to the one at Ephesus. The latter had *left off* its *initial love* even as the former had become *lukewarm* — both no doubt represent second-generation communities in which the spiritual fires had burned low!

Laodicea presents us for the first time in Christian history with the picture of a *rich* church. Most early Greek Christians had been slaves drawn from estates of the Roman nobility (I Cor. 1:26 ff.). Few like Philemon themselves held slaves. Now, in a later period we may observe the first *wealthy* church having *no need of anything!* The sarcasm descriptive of this church's real *poverty* abounds in references to the manufactures and trade of this opulent city.

Probably few recall, as they gaze at Holman Hunt's suggestive painting, that it is the *door* of this rich church at Laodicea — overgrown with the *thorns* of *the cares of this world and the delight in riches* (Matt. 13:22) — upon which " The Light of the World " is knocking!

This first act of our drama ends with the gracious promise that those who open to this Lord of Life will experience the rich fellowship so often described in Scripture in terms of the Kingdom banquet (Ps. 23; Isa., ch. 55; Luke 13:29). Again, the *victor* in the world's moral strife is to occupy his Lord's *throne* with him, thus fulfilling God's initial purpose that man should have dominion over all his creation (Gen. 1:28). This privilege man's Lord can promise his followers because he is himself *the Beginning* — that is, the mediate instrument in the fashioning — *of God's creation* (Col. 1:15).

And so the curtain falls on Act I.

# Act II

## VISION OF GOD IN HEAVEN

### God's Purpose in History

(Chs. 4:1 to 8:1)

*Stage Setting:* The Throne of God (4:1–8a); The Odes of Creatures and Elders (4:8b–11); The Book and the Lamb (5:1–7); The Three Hymns (5:8–14)

#### THE OPENING OF THE SEVEN SEALS (6:1 to 8:1)

Scene 1  The Rider on the White Horse: Conquest (6:1, 2)

Scene 2  The Rider on the Red Horse: Civil War (6:3, 4)

Scene 3  The Rider on the Black Horse: Famine (6:5, 6)

Scene 4  The Rider on the Yellow Horse: Death (6:7, 8)

Scene 5  The Prayer of the Martyrs Beneath the Altar (6:9–11)

Scene 6  The Eschatological Events (6:12 to 7:17)

      a. Cosmic Catastrophies (6:12–17)

      b. Sealing of the Martyrs (7:1–8)

      c. The Martyrs in Heaven (7:9–17)

Scene 7  Silence in Heaven (8:1)

*Stage Setting: The Throne of God (4:1–8a); The Odes of Creatures and Elders (4:8b–11); The Book and the Lamb (5:1–7); The Three Hymns (5:8–14)*

(With the opening of Act II the action shifts to the eternal realm. In the middle of the stage appears the throne of God. Twenty-four other seats are arranged on either side in the form of a semicircle. Before the throne appear the Lamb, candelabra, and crystal sea. Characters include the twenty-four elders, four creatures, and at one side the narrator.)

*As before, John speaks —*

After this I had another vision. Lo! there was a door open in heaven and the former voice which I had heard speaking with me — the one like a trumpet — was saying: "Come up here. I shall show you the things that are certain to happen hereafter." I came at once under the Spirit's influence.

### The Throne of God

Lo! a throne was set up in heaven. Upon the throne there was One sitting — he who sat was for inscrutableness like a translucent stone (jasper or sard). A semicircle, rainbow-shaped, ran out from the throne on either side — emerald-green it appeared to the eye. On this semicircle on either side of the throne twenty-four seats were arranged. Upon these seats sat twenty-four elders arrayed in white robes and with golden crowns on their heads.

Out of the throne there proceeded lightning, voices, and peals of thunder.

Before the throne burned seven flaming lamps — these are the seven spirits of God. Also before the throne was what appeared like a sea of glass, crystalline for clarity.

In the space before and around the throne were four creatures which were full of eyes inside and out. The first creature was like a lion, the second like an ox, the third had a face like a man, the fourth appeared like an eagle in flight. The four creatures had six wings each — these too were full of eyes around and within. (4:1–8a)

WITH ACT II a complete shift of scenery occurs. Act I had pictured the Church on earth — its spiritual and moral warfare there, its Redeemer and Lord in its midst earnestly striving for its salvation. Act II takes us at once — through *a door open in heaven* — into the higher realm of God's eternal order.

It is the *voice . . . like a trumpet* which John had heard at the beginning (1:10) that is in command throughout the drama. This is the voice of the *Son of Man*. When an angel addresses the seer it is as this Son of Man's emissary and at his behest. He has equal authority on earth and in heaven, for he is man's only Lord (Phil. 2:10 f.).

The *throne* of God is henceforth the principal prop on the stage. In this respect John's drama is akin to all the apocalypses. God is sovereign over all creation — such is its import. In tabernacle and temple God's throne was the portion of the lid of the Ark of the Covenant between the worshiping cherubim. As the Ark stood in the inner part of the sanctuary (the " Holy of Holies "), it is clear that John visualizes the open sanctuary as always present on this heavenly stage.

The *twenty-four seats* for the *elders* were set up after the mode of the Jewish Sanhedrin in *a semicircle* about the throne. These elders represent the Church, which sits in rule or judgment over men and history (Luke 22:30; Rev. 3:21). The physical phenomena proceeding from the throne express God's power and majesty (Ex. 19:16 ff.). The *seven flaming lamps* here stand for the Spirit of God, as did the seven-branched candlestick of the tabernacle (Zech. 4:2 ff.). The *sea* is the laver of the latter (Ex. 30:17 ff.) — symbol of that purity without which man cannot approach God. The *four creatures* represent all creation and their *eyes* God's intimate knowledge of all his works (Ezek. 1:5 ff.).

### ODE OF THE FOUR CREATURES

The four creatures chant continually day and night —

> "Holy, holy, holy,
> Lord God Almighty,
> Who was and who is and who comes."

### ODE OF THE TWENTY-FOUR ELDERS

Whenever the creatures ascribe glory, honor, and thanksgiving to the Occupant of the throne who lives eternally, the twenty-four elders fall down before him — they worship him who lives forever — they cast their crowns before the throne, chanting —

> "Worthy art thou,
> O Lord our God,
> To receive glory, praise, and power,
> For thou didst create all things;
> By thy will they have been — yea, they were created."

(4:8b–11)

### THE SEALED BOOK

I observed in the right hand of the Occupant of the throne a Book written both within and without and sealed with seven seals. I saw also a mighty angel who was announcing with a strong voice, "Who is worthy to open the Book and to loose its seals?"

No one in either heaven or earth — or beneath the earth even — was found capable of opening the Book or of looking at it. I wept copiously because none worthy to open the Book or to look at it was to be found. Then one of the elders said to me: "Weep not. Look — the Lion of the tribe of Judah, the Root of David, has gained the victory required to open the Book and its seven seals."

Then I beheld, in the space bounded by the throne, the four creatures, and the elders, a Lamb standing though it had the look of having been slaughtered. It had seven horns and seven eyes — the latter being the seven spirits of God which are sent out into all the earth. This Lamb came and took the Book from the right hand of the throne's Occupant. (5:1–7)

W<small>E ARE</small> still concerned here with stage props. As in most of the acts of this drama, considerable activity in heaven forms part of the background for the action depicted in the succeeding scenes. This is merely John's way of saying that the events of history and of man's salvation must be viewed in the light of God's redemptive purpose and industry.

The *four creatures chant* a hymn of praise to God. That is, all creation by virtue of its beauty and inherent worth radiates the splendor of its Maker — for he made it what it is — he is the skilled Artisan who wrought it at his forge. This is a familiar Biblical conception (Ps. 8; 19:1–6; 104). The *twenty-four elders* (the Church) have the insight to discern nature's witness to its Maker, as their ode suggests. Thus, with two odes John gives expression to the two thoughts of nature's constant eulogy to its Creator and of Spirit-filled humanity's ability to penetrate nature's veil and see God behind it.

The *Book* with the *seven seals* contains God's purpose in history, as will appear when the seals are broken. To *open the Book and its seven seals* means to bring this purpose to fulfillment — this cannot be achieved save by one who *has gained the victory* upon which such fulfillment is predicated. Jesus Christ has done this — he is the " star " in this drama — he it is who fulfills the ultimate will of God for man, who achieves his final purpose in creating his universe. Paradoxically, he is symbolized by both *Lion* and *Lamb* as elsewhere in Scripture (Gen. 49:9 f.; John 1:29) — his power is that of self-denying love. His *seven horns* indicate might; his *seven eyes,* the moral insight which is that of God's Spirit.

*Stage Setting* (Continued)

### Hymn of Creation and the Church

Now when the Lamb took the Book, the four creatures and the twenty-four elders fell down before him. Each had a harp and a golden bowl full of incense representing the prayers of the saints. And they sang a new hymn —

> "Worthy art thou to receive the Book and open its seals,
> For thou hast been slaughtered,
> And thou hast bought with thy blood for God
> Some from every tribe and tongue and people and race —
> A kingdom and priests to our God hast thou made them;
> Upon earth shall they reign."

### Hymn of the Hosts of Heaven

I beheld yet more. I heard the voices of many angels about the throne, the creatures, and the elders — their number was thousands of thousands and ten thousands of ten thousands. What they chanted with a mighty shout was —

> "Worthy is the slaughtered Lamb
> Of receiving
> Power, riches, wisdom, might,
> Honor, glory, and praise."

### Hymn of All Creation

And all creation — everything in heaven, on earth, under the earth, and in the sea (indeed, this whole universe) — I heard chanting —

> "To the Occupant of the throne
> And to the Lamb
> Be ascribed
> Praise, honor, glory, and might,
> Forever and ever."

Then the four creatures responded, "Amen."
And the elders fell down in worship.

(5:8–14)

THE THREE HYMNS on this page complete the setting for Act II. Collectively they represent the praise of the *Lamb* as sung by all of God's creatures — whether of *heaven* or *earth* or *sea*. Such worship is his due because by his death (*thou hast been slaughtered . . . bought with thy blood*) God's final purpose for man and for his redemption has been achieved.

The first hymn is sung jointly by the *four creatures* as typical of all beings of God's making and the *twenty-four elders* — the Church in its triumphant state, *a kingdom* wherein *they reign* with God. During the hymn, the elders offer up *bowls full of incense — the prayers of the saints* (Ps. 141:2) — thus discharging the Church's function as *priests*. The universal nature of the salvation which God offers through the Lamb is clearly expressed in the words of the hymn. Later as the *seals* are opened, it will become evident that this formation of the saved people of God is the consummation of his ultimate purpose for man.

In the second hymn the hosts of heaven are heard eternally chanting the *praise* of the Lamb. The stress lies on his worthiness. This is the result of his readiness to be *slaughtered* that God's saving intent relative to man may be achieved.

The third hymn is a grand finale in which all of God's creatures in *heaven, earth,* and *sea* ascribe to him and to the Lamb the praise that is their due. The imagination is staggered by the vision of a stage so large as to accommodate all creation!

What a penetrating view this stage setting affords of God and his world! In ch. 4 we see him sitting in awful majesty surrounded by his creatures and his Church. Chapter 5, then, introduces the Book of the Divine Plan, the Lamb by whose labors it is accomplished, and the worshiping hosts. A cosmic setting for our drama, indeed!

## Scene 1

### THE RIDER ON THE WHITE HORSE: *Conquest*

I watched while the Lamb loosed the first of the seven seals. Then I listened as with a voice like thunder one of the four creatures shouted, "Come forth."

I looked — lo! it was a white horse. Its rider had a bow. A crown, too, was given him. He rode out as a conqueror bent on further victories! (6:1, 2)

## Scene 2

### THE RIDER ON THE RED HORSE: *Civil War*

When the Lamb loosed the second seal, I heard the second creature shout, "Come forth."

Then there came out another horse — a red one. For him who sat astride it was found opportunity to rob earth of peace and instigate men to the killing of each other. So he was presented with a huge sword! (6:3, 4)

## Scene 3

### THE RIDER ON THE BLACK HORSE: *Famine*

When the Lamb loosed the third seal, I heard the third creature shout, "Come forth."

Lo! this was a black horse. Its rider had a pair of scales in his hand.

Then I heard a voice, issuing — so it seemed — from among the four creatures, which said: "A quart of wheat at a denarius and three quarts of barley at the same. But do not decrease the quantity of oil and wine." (6:5, 6)

## Scene 4

### THE RIDER ON THE YELLOW HORSE: *Death*

When the Lamb loosed the fourth seal, I heard the voice of the fourth creature as he shouted, "Come forth."

Again I watched and lo! it was a yellow horse. He that sat upon it — his name was *Death* — and the *Grave* followed him!

For them was found "authority" over a fourth part of earth — authorization to slay with the sword, with famine, with death, and by means of earth's beasts. (6:7, 8)

BEFORE THE SANCTUARY with its throne and in full sight of the hosts gathered on our cosmic stage as " supers " for Act II, there follow in rapid succession four scenes that together tell a dismal tale. It is the sad story of man's frustrations and of the futility of his labors; it is the cyclic rumble of the rise and fall of cultures and civilizations.

Hard upon the discovery of any land or continent, there comes conquest — the *rider* on the *white horse* enters the land *as a conquerer* and he reckons up *his victories* in terms of the multitudes of the slain. Then with the exploitation of the land's resources, followed by increase in riches, men's jealousies and lusts are aroused — with the result that civil war stalks across the land and the envious and self-indulgent *instigate men to the killing of each other.* Always the net product of man's wars is poverty, disease, and famine. Then it is the poor — whose staple diet is *wheat* or rice or *barley* — that are hardest hit; the rich, with their passion for *oil* and *wine,* are little affected by these hardships. In the end *Death* and *the Grave* walk sadly through the land — men die, cultures die, civilizations pass away, buried beneath the sands and floods.

Such is the story of humanity " without God in the world " — a ghastly epic it is of endlessly recurring vanity, ineptitude, triviality, futility, nihilism, despair! Such is the account of what man left to his own devices can bring forth in that garden of earth wherein God has granted his wisdom and power free scope to display what they can do! Hinduism's doctrine of countless cycles of incarnations — though doubtless of little worth as regards the individual's life and destiny — affords a true insight into the history of man's life on the racial and cultural levels.

Collectively the Four Horsemen of the Apocalypse compose a realistic picture of man's tragic incompetence and melancholy end!

## THE PRAYER OF THE MARTYRS BENEATH THE ALTAR

When the Lamb loosed the fifth seal, I beheld beneath the altar of sacrifice the souls of those who have been slaughtered on account of the Word of God — because, that is, of the witness which they have given to it.

These shouted with a loud voice, saying —

> " O holy and faithful Master,
> How long —
> Wilt thou not render judgment and avenge our blood
> On the denizens of earth? "

Then to each of them was given a white flowing robe and they were told to be patient yet a little while — only till the company of their compatriots and brothers, who were about to be liquidated even as they, should be made up! (6:9–11)

THIS SCENE and the series of four preceding it are in startling contrast. The curtain has been run up and down rapidly four times upon four deeply moving tableaux — scenes that depicted the entire gamut of man's devastating experience of wasted opportunity and hopeless end. But man's true destiny is not the grave, nor is death necessarily his final victor.

Scene 5 is intended in the first instance to make this clear. For those dead who have been *slaughtered* for the *Word of God* the end is not yet. Death for such is not an end but a beginning. They are not destined to lie forever *beneath the altar of sacrifice* — they will rise again (I Cor. 15:20 ff.)!

Impatient of vindication — even of retribution — the martyrs no doubt are. (John is here indulging in a piece of Christian surrealism to get across the point that God will surely vindicate his righteous reign in the world and therewith those who have been faithful to him.) Now, God's kind of vindication will come in due time — after all his faithful witnesses have been *liquidated*. In the meantime, each martyr is *given* the *white flowing robe* of righteousness — the " court dress " of the heavenly throne room — sufficient justification for him if he will but stop a moment to consider! Who but the nobility of the realm are presented in proper garb to the King?

This scene gains in impressiveness when it is recalled that the Greek word *martyr* means simply " a witness." All faithful Christians are martyrs in the Greek sense and potential " martyrs " in that which the word has acquired in English. It is highly probable, then, that John thinks of the whole Church as lying *slaughtered* for its witness to the Word, in contrast with mankind generally — brought low in death and the grave through man's own senseless futility.

## Scene 6

# THE ESCHATOLOGICAL EVENTS
### (6:12 to 7:17)

### a. Cosmic Catastrophies

Now I observed that when the Lamb loosed the sixth seal there was a terrific earthquake. The sun was darkened — it took on the appearance of hairy sackcloth. The round moon looked like a single drop of blood. The stars fell from sky to earth — it seemed as though a fig tree were dropping its unripe figs under the lashing of a strong wind. Even the heavens were driven afar just like a scroll that is being rolled up. Every mountain and island was jarred out of its place.

Then the kings of earth, the nobility, the "colonels," the wealthy and powerful, together with every slave and freeman, hid themselves in caves and rocks in the mountains. And to the mountains and rocks they cried: "Fall upon us! Cover us up! — away from the Presence of the Occupant of the throne, away from the Lamb's wrath! For the Great Day of their wrath has come! — and who can take it?" (6:12–17)

### b. Sealing of the Martyrs

I saw next four angels standing at the four corners of earth. They were restraining earth's four winds lest they blow on earth and sea, and particularly upon the vegetation.

Then I beheld another angel coming up from the east. He was the bearer of the seal of the living God.

He shouted with a lusty voice to the four angels to whom was entrusted the harming of earth and sea, "Do no hurt to earth or sea or vegetation — not until we stamp God's seal upon the foreheads of his servants."

Moreover, I heard the count of those who were then sealed — one hundred, forty-four thousand it was — sealed they were out of every tribe of the "sons of Israel." Twelve thousand were sealed respectively from the tribes of Judah, Reuben, Gad, Asher, Naphtali, Manasseh, Simeon, Levi, Issachar, Zebulun, Joseph, and Benjamin. (7:1–8)

FOLLOWING the two contrasting spectacles of death which were displayed so forcibly in Scenes 1 through 5, we now behold the final denouement. It is the eschatological time — the " day " of the last things. It is the cosmic " V Day " — a very narrow slit of time combining historical and eternal periods of existence. In this relatively short epoch God must vindicate his creation of and Lordship over nature and man!

The entire universe is to be affected by this transition — it is an event of cosmic significance. Accordingly, John — in terms borrowed largely from the Hebrew prophets — describes its effects on *sun* and *moon,* the *stars* and *heavens,* and upon the *mountains* and *islands* of the earth (Isa. 13:10; 34:4; Ezek. 32:7). These cosmic events are not to be taken too seriously for their own sakes. They are intended largely as background for the seer's major interest — the fate of all classes and conditions of men in God's final purpose.

This is shown to be of two kinds. There are, first, those among mankind who have consistently rejected their Maker and his Lordship over their lives. These can only flee from his *Presence* and from the *wrath* of his appointed representative, the *Lamb.*

The second group — the faithful *servants* of the *living God* — have his *seal* placed upon them, the symbol in Scripture of God's purpose to save or to protect (Ezek. 9:4, 6). They are not to be *hurt* by *earth's* traditional *four winds* (Zech. 6:5) — that is, by any evil which the harsh world and its secular powers can bring to bear upon mankind.

Who, then, are these *servants* of God? For the moment they are defined in terms of the older " *sons of Israel* " and the traditional twelve *tribes* — the people of God in a former generation — but the Church applied this older terminology to itself (Gal. 6:16; I Peter 1:1 f.).

## c. The Martyrs in Heaven

Again I looked — lo! there was a huge multitude which no one was able to count — they were of every race, from all tribes, peoples, and tongues. They were standing before the throne and the Lamb. Clothed in white flowing robes they were, with palm branches in their hands.

### Hymn of the Redeemed

They were shouting with a mighty voice —

> "Salvation is our God's possession,
> His who occupies the throne
> And the Lamb's."

### Hymn of the Heavenly Hosts

Then all the angels gathered about the throne, the elders, and the four creatures, and fell down on their faces before the throne and worshiped God, chanting —

> "Amen.
> Praise, glory, wisdom, thanksgiving,
> Honor, power, and might
> To our God forever and ever.
> Amen."

Then one of the elders inquired of me, "These who wear the white flowing robes — who are they and from where do they come?"
I replied, "My lord, thou knowest."
He answered me: "These are they who come out of the *Great Tribulation*. They have washed their robes and have bleached them white in the blood of the Lamb. This is the reason that they are to be found before the throne of God. They are to serve him night and day in his sanctuary and the Occupant of the throne will dwell with them. They will never hunger again nor thirst any more, nor will the sun smite them nor any heat overcome them. For the Lamb who is before the throne will shepherd them — he will guide their way to springs of Water of Life. God, moreover, will wipe away every tear from their eyes." (7:9–17)

THE ACTION in this sixth scene is both swift and paradoxical. A moment ago we were watching the events of the cosmic "V Day" and their effects on nature and man in an earthly setting. Now, in a trice we are asked to look away from earth to heaven, to observe a vast *multitude* congregating before the *throne* of God in the heavenly sanctuary.

Who, then, are these? They are once again the assembly of the martyrs — the *slaughtered* whom in Scene 5 we saw lying *beneath the altar of sacrifice* — as their wearing the court dress (*white flowing robes*) and being presented to the King clearly signify. Too, they are the *sealed* of the present scene — those who have come out of the *Great Tribulation* of "V Day." Hence, we make the equation: *slaughtered* (martyrs) = "*sons of Israel*" = the Christian Church, in John's vocabulary.

This is the final resurrection — the ultimate victory over *death* and *the grave* for which we have been looking. It was with a view to this denouement that the universe — and particularly man — was created. God has all along been in the business of making men — "sons of God" (Rom. 8:19 — "son of" being a Semitic idiom meaning "like"; hence, "men like God") — men like himself in moral character, in righteousness, purity, truth, love, and essential goodness — men worthy of wearing the court dress of righteousness like God's own!

And how was this handiwork of God accomplished? By what "master stroke" did he bring such "sons" into being? By *washing their robes* and *bleaching them white in the blood of the Lamb* — such is the seer's answer to these questions. Figurative language aside, God achieved his saving purpose by appointing for men a "Captain of their salvation" (Heb. 2:10) — a Leader through whose efforts they have been formed into a moral community of high integrity and character, worthy of fellowship with the living God.

## SCENE 7
### SILENCE IN HEAVEN

When the Lamb loosed the seventh seal,
Silence reigned in heaven
Half an hour, so to speak.

(8:1)

IN THE LANGUAGE of this drama, a short measure of time indicates a transition period, a brief pause before events of great significance, a short epoch of no lasting importance, or an impatient reference to a space of time a detailed narration of whose events is to be made in later scenes (2:9; 11:2, 3, 11; 12:6). The *half an hour* of the present scene is of the last-named type. For a brief moment heaven's clock is stopped, so to speak — the swift action on this cosmic stage is " frozen," the actors all stand, as in the fairy story of the " sleeping beauty" and her attendants, dormant in their tracks!

This is a *silence* that can be " felt." It is breath-taking in its suggestiveness — clearly this cannot be the end of the drama. It is only that for the moment time and eternity appear to stand still — surely there is more to come.

What a marvelous display of John's literary art this is in reality! How better could our spiritual appetites be whetted for what is to follow?

The curtain comes down on Act II after this *half an hour* in which its " frozen " actors have stood immobile before us, the scene etched indelibly on our memories. But what, we ask, can be the real content and contribution of Scene 7 to the drama as a whole? Was there perchance something there upon the stage — some significant detail, some item of cosmic import — that we have missed? Well, we had that *half an hour* to discover it! But we need not be too distressed if we have failed to observe it now; we may rest assured that succeeding scenes will make it plain to us. For this is John's artistry at work!

## Act

## III

# VISION OF THE SEVEN ANGELS OF THE PRESENCE

*The Church in Tribulation*

(Chs. 8:2 to 11:18)

*Stage Setting:* The Altars and the Angel with the Prayers of the Saints (8:2-6)

### THE SOUNDING OF THE SEVEN TRUMPETS (8:7 to 11:18)

Scene 1    Hail and Fire Fall on the Earth (8:7)

Scene 2    A Mountain Cast Into the Sea (8:8, 9)

Scene 3    A Great Star Falls on Rivers and Springs (8:10, 11)

Scene 4    Heavenly Bodies Darkened (8:12)

### AN EAGLE ANNOUNCES THREE WOES (8:13)

Scene 5    (Woe 1) The Pit of the Abyss Opened: Locusts (9:1-12)

Scene 6    (Woe 2) Release of the Four Angels on the Euphrates (9:13-15); The Two Hundred Million Horsemen (9:16-21); The Strong Angel with the Little Book (10:1-11); The "Times of the Gentiles," The Two Prophets, The Evil City (Sodom, Egypt) (11:1-14)

Scene 7    (Woe 3) Worship in Heaven (11:15-18)

## Stage Setting: The Altars and the Angel with the Prayers of the Saints
### (8:2–6)

(The stage again shows the open sanctuary. Prominently displayed are the altars of sacrifice and of incense. An angel stands at the former as the curtain is run up. Before the throne are also the seven angels of the Presence, each with a trumpet in hand.)

*The narrator opens with* —

I beheld the seven angels who stand continuously in the Presence of God, while seven trumpets were distributed among them.

Then another angel came and took his stand at the altar of sacrifice holding a golden censer in his hand. Incense in considerable amount was given him with a view to his placing it on the golden altar before the throne. This he was to do while all the saints offered their prayers.

So at this angel's hand the smoke of the incense arose before God as the saints prayed. Afterward the angel took the censer, filled it with the burning mass from off the golden altar, and threw it to earth. The result — claps of thunder, voices, lightning, and an earthquake!

Then the seven angels holding the seven trumpets prepared to blow them. (8:2–6)

THE CHURCH at prayer is the spectacle that greets our eyes as the curtain rises on Act III! It is the hour of morning sacrifice in the heavenly sanctuary — it cannot well be that of the other appointed hour (evening), for there is *no night* in heaven (21:25). Indeed, it is the exact moment when an *angel* (in lieu of the usual priest chosen for the day) is approaching the *golden altar* to offer up the *incense* symbolical of the *prayers* of God's people (Ps. 141:2). *Before the throne* — showing as before in the open sanctuary — is seen the kneeling congregation of the *saints.*

As in Scene 5 of Act II, this spectacle of a worshiping and trusting people is intended to produce an atmosphere on stage calculated to condition us properly for the catastrophic events of the "last times" about to be displayed. There it was the *slaughtered* (martyrs), here the *saints,* who are seen at prayer. But we have seen reason to believe that for the seer these represent the same group — namely, the Church Universal — for the *saints* are all potentially martyrs through that commitment which accompanies confession of Jesus Christ as Lord of Life.

The use of *trumpets* to signalize the opening of the epoch of the "last things" is traditional (Isa. 27:13; Matt. 24:31). It is quite natural, too, that the *seven angels* of the *Presence* — archangels in some of the apocalypses, and in any case God's heralds who do his bidding — should be assigned this task. That the *angel* throws part of *the burning mass* of incense *from off the golden altar* down *to earth* and its attendant effect (*thunder, voices, lightning, earthquake*) signify a causal relation between the Church's *prayers* and the working out of the divine plan in the scenes that immediately follow.

## HAIL AND FIRE FALL ON THE EARTH

The first angel blew. Then hail and fire mingled with blood rained to earth. So a third of the earth, including a third of its plant life, was consumed — indeed, all the green grass was burnt off. (8:7)

### Scene 2

## A MOUNTAIN CAST INTO THE SEA

The second angel blew, when what appeared to be a huge mountain burning and fiery red fell into the sea. As a result a third part of the sea turned bloody, a third of the creatures inhabiting the sea — its living colony — died, a third of its ships were destroyed. (8:8, 9)

### Scene 3

## A GREAT STAR FALLS ON RIVERS AND SPRINGS

The third angel blew and there fell from the sky a brilliant star burning like a lamp. Its fall affected a third of all rivers and springs of water. The star's name was Apsynthus (Wormwood). So a third of all waters became wormwood-like and, because of the waters being embittered with the poison, many people died. (8:10, 11)

### Scene 4

## HEAVENLY BODIES DARKENED

The fourth angel blew. At this a third part of the sun, the moon, and the stars was affected. That third of each of them was extinguished, so that daytime was diminished by a third, and nighttime likewise. (8:12)

FROM THIS THIRD ACT of the drama to its end we have to do only with the events of the eschatological period. The Four Horsemen never again appear on John's cosmic stage, nor is there further development of the idea they represent — man's utter futility and hopeless end. In other words, history without God holds no lasting interest for this prophet. His theme is rather the entrance of God onto the plane of history and the shattering results of the same for the world of nature and of man.

Essentially the happenings of Scenes 1 to 4 on the page opposite are an elaboration of the " cosmic catastrophies " of Scene 6 in Act II above (p. 52). This same series of events will again recur in Act V (Scenes 1 to 4) which runs parallel to the one before us. Indeed, this is perhaps the place to remark that Acts III and IV, and V and VI form two couplets, all of which are merely elaborations of the eschatological motif first presented in Scene 6 of Act II. The first couplet will be seen to picture the way in which the Church " weathers the gale " in these devastating times, and similarly the second couplet will depict the secular world's failure to do so.

In general, it will be noted that only *a third* of creation in its various parts (*earth, sea, rivers and springs,* heavenly bodies) is to be affected by the disasters described on the page opposite. This means that the final end of all things has not yet arrived. The plagues mentioned in Scenes 1, 2, and 4 find their origin in the account of the Exodus (Ex. 9:23–26; 7:20 f.; 10:21). The fall of the *brilliant star* in Scene 3 has a parallel at Isa. 14:12. For John *star* means an angel (cf. 1:20; 9:1 ff.) — in this case, a " fallen " angel identified with a well-known *poison* (Jer. 9:15; 23:15) and so harmful to man, as the other plagues here are not.

# AN EAGLE ANNOUNCES THREE WOES

*John proceeds —*

I observed further. Then I heard an eagle as it flew in mid-sky announcing with a mighty shout: "Woe! Woe! Woe!" — for what is about to befall earth's inhabitants when the three angels who are left sound the remaining trumpet blasts! (8:13)

## SCENE 5 (*Woe I*)
### THE PIT OF THE ABYSS OPENED: *Locusts*

The fifth angel blew and I beheld a star fallen from sky to earth. The key of the pit of the abyss was given him. He opened the pit of the abyss and smoke like that of an enormous furnace rose out of it. Thereupon sun and air were blackened by the pit's smoke.

Out of the smoke there came locusts upon the earth. These were permitted the sort of destructive power possessed by earth's scorpions. Only they were told not to harm the grass of the field nor other greenery and plant life, but rather those people failing to have on their foreheads the seal of God. They were not allowed, moreover, to slay such, but merely to torment them throughout five months. (Their manner of tormenting was like that of a scorpion when it stings a man.)

In those days men will court death and not attain it — they will long to die and death will fly from them!

The appearance of these locusts was like horses panoplied for war. On their heads were crown-shaped forms resembling gold — their faces were like those of men — they had hair such as women have — their teeth resembled those of lions — their chests looked like iron breastplates — the sound of their wings approached the noise of chariots drawn by many horses and rushing into battle. Tails they had like those of scorpions and the stings to match — it was in these tails that their power to hurt men for five months resided.

As king over them the locusts have the angel of the abyss — his name in Hebrew is *Abaddon,* and in Greek, *Apollyon* (the Destroyer).

The first Woe has passed. Look — there are yet two Woes to come hereafter. (9:1–12)

THIS SERIES of three *Woes* is intended as a warning to all peoples. It is the negative side of the gospel message (Luke 6:24–26). Its purpose is to bring all men to repentance, as is clearly stated in 9:20 f. It is the final exhibition of God's wish to save all (I Tim. 2:3 f.).

In Scene 6 of Act II we beheld the multitude of those who *have on their foreheads the seal of God*. But thus far we have not been enlightened as to the nature of the *Great Tribulation* through which they are to pass. We now begin to have this depicted for us. It is to be a period during which an immoral *destructive power* under its leader, *Apollyon,* will arise from the underworld (*the pit of the abyss*). That these *locusts* symbolize a force of an immoral type is clear. They have no power to *harm the grass* or other *plant life* like ordinary locusts. The evil they achieve is rather in the realm of the spirit or of human personality. This, then, is a graphic picture of the immoral influences which man finds at work in his world and surrounding him. It is the Sin of the Race in its corporate capacity — it arises like *smoke* from the *pit* to swarm round the individual and *torment* him, but it cannot *slay* him. The individual's moral death can be brought about only by his yielding to the onslaught of this horde, by self-destruction!

The evil of this ghastly crew never gets out of hand. It is somehow under God's sovereign control. The period of its activity is limited to *five months* — a very short time in the language of apocalyptic.

This invasion of locusts from the abyss was no doubt suggested by that depicted in Joel, chs. 1 and 2 where the same motif of repentance is in view (see Ex. 10:12 ff.). As in Joel, both God's people and the pagan world undergo this *torment,* but with quite differing feelings and attitudes and hence with opposing results on character.

## Scene 6 (*Woe II*)

## RELEASE OF THE FOUR ANGELS ON THE EUPHRATES

The sixth angel blew. Then I heard a voice issuing from the four horns of the golden altar which stands before God. It said to the sixth angel holding a trumpet, " Release the four angels that stand bound on the banks of the mighty river Euphrates." So the four angels were loosed who had been readied for the exact hour, day, month, and year to slaughter a third part of mankind. (9:13-15)

### THE TWO HUNDRED MILLION HORSEMEN

The number of their horsemen was two hundred million — I heard the count reported. As I beheld the horses and their riders in the vision, they appeared to have breastplates of fiery red, hyacinth, and a sulphureous hue — the horses' heads were like those of lions — out of their mouths proceeded fire, smoke, and brimstone. By these three plagues a third of mankind were slain — that is, by the fire, smoke, and brimstone proceeding from their mouths. For the destructive power of the horses lay in both their mouths and their tails. Their tails, indeed, were like serpents — they possessed heads and they could inflict hurt with them.

The rest of mankind who were not slain by these plagues failed to repent of the works of their hands. Rather they continued their worshiping of demigods and of idols of gold and silver, of brass, wood, and stone — idols which can neither see nor hear nor move about. Nor did they repent of their murders, their sorceries, their fornications, and their thievings. (9:16-21)

WITH *the second Woe* we are given still more detail with which to fill in the cryptic narrative of the "last times" found in Scene 6 of Act II. The *four angels* here are certainly to be identified with those *standing at the four corners of earth* in that scene. There they are the guardians of *earth's four winds;* here, the leaders of a vast troop.

Some have suggested that these *horsemen* represent the Parthian or other hordes out of the east feared in John's day. But this is not to penetrate to the depth of his message and its universal application. Moreover it destroys the symbolism, reducing the book's dramatic metaphor to the level of shallow prose. It is more probable by far that the seer's mind still dwells on the imagery of the prophet Joel, which suggested the *locusts* of *the first Woe*. In the older prophet that plague was followed by a gathering of "all the men of war" of the nations to do battle against the Lord and his hosts (3:9 ff.). It can scarcely be without intent that we find the same sequence here — first, locusts; then, a horde of warriors. John's *horsemen,* then, will symbolize the secular might of a world culture dedicated to the endeavor to destroy God's rule over the lives of men.

As before, the power of evil is restricted — only *a third of mankind* will be slain — such is God's decree. Still, *the rest of mankind* remain wedded to their idols — not even fear of evil can force men to enter the Kingdom of Heaven!

That the action of this scene is set in motion by *a voice issuing from . . . the golden altar* of incense substantiates what has been said of the causal relation existing between prayer and the working out of the eschatological drama (p. 61). The exactness of the time element suggested by the reference to *hour, day, month, and year* indicates again that the entire drama is within the plan and authority of God (Mark 13:32).

I beheld, then, another angel — a mighty one — descending out of the sky. He was swathed in a cloud — a rainbow upon his head — his countenance like the sun — his legs resembling pillars of fire. He had a little book open in his hand. He planted his right foot on the sea, his left on the land, and shouted out in a huge voice like a lion roaring. When he cried out, seven thunders crashed. As the seven thunders boomed forth, I was on the point of writing. But I heard a voice out of heaven saying: "Seal up what the seven thunders have said. Do not write down these things."

Moreover, the angel that I saw standing on sea and land raised his right hand toward heaven and swore by Him who lives forever and ever and who created heaven and earth and sea, together with everything in them: "There will be no more delay. But as soon as the seventh angel blows — rather in the days following his blast — God's Mystery will be brought to its fruition, just as he promised his servants, the prophets."

Then again the voice which I had been hearing out of heaven began to speak with me. "Go," it was saying, "take the book open in the angel's hand as he stands there on sea and land." So I went up to the angel, saying to him that he should give me the little book.

He replied to me: "Take it and eat it up. It will embitter your stomach but prove sweet as honey in your mouth!"

So I took the little book from the angel's hand and proceeded to devour it. It was, indeed, as sweet as honey in my mouth. But when I had finished eating it, my stomach became bitter!

Then they said to me, "It is imperative that you prophesy further regarding many peoples, nations, tongues, and kings." (10:1–11)

THIS INCIDENT of the " strong angel " forms a fascinating interlude in John's drama. For the first and last time the seer is drawn away from his observer's corner to the very center of the stage! This is akin to the magician's choice of an individual from his audience to serve as a momentary buffer to his act. For a brief time the prophet himself holds our interest in the very scene that he is narrating!

On second thought, however, it becomes obvious that this by-play had to occur at least once. Otherwise it would have remained unclear just how John and his fellow evangelists dedicated to the gospel's proclamation are related to this cosmic drama.

John is the typical evangelist and his book is a piece — and for its day a very powerful piece, indeed — of evangelistic publicity. In this scene, accordingly, in most engaging fashion the *imperative* nature of his labors for the gospel's effective presentation is set forth. So Paul in both Colossians (1:24 to 2:5) and Ephesians (3:1–13) does not hesitate to stress the importance of his efforts to bring the gospel to a needy world and Church.

Now, the evangelist's task is a never-ending one. At times he is overeager to have done with it. The *seven thunders* contain God's last Word, so to speak, as their title indicates (see 4:5 and 11:19), and John would gladly *write down* their content and draw his drama to a close. But it is only halfway through! God is very gracious and patient with mankind, and in the *little book* of his purposes there is much yet to be done and said and written for the saving of *peoples, nations, tongues, and kings.* Much of this will appear *bitter* for God's prophets to assimilate — however agreeable and *sweet* its over-all message may be at first blush — for it involves persecution and sorrow for God's people, as we shall see (Zech. 2:8).

## THE "TIMES OF THE GENTILES," THE TWO PROPHETS, THE EVIL CITY (SODOM, EGYPT)

After this I was handed a measuring rod like a cane and I was told: "Rise up. Measure the sanctuary of God, the altar, and those who worship there. But the courtyard outside the sanctuary leave out — do not measure it! For it has been given over to the nations and they will tramp the Holy City for forty-two months. Moreover, I shall commit the responsibility for it to my two witnesses, who garbed in sackcloth will preach in it for a thousand, two hundred, and sixty days."

These witnesses are the two olive trees and lampstands which stand continuously before the Lord of earth. If anyone seeks to harm them, fire issues from their mouths and devours such enemies. Indeed, such is the decreed manner of his slaying, if anyone should wish to harm them.

They have the power to close up the sky, so that it may not rain during the period of their preaching. Moreover, they have delegated authority over the waters to transform them into blood and over the land to smite it with a mighty plague of their own choosing.

When they complete their witnessing, the Beast that comes up from the abyss will engage them in battle; he will overcome and slay them. Then their corpses will lie exposed on the broad thoroughfare of the Great City which is known allegorically as *Sodom* and *Egypt* — that city in which their Lord was crucified. Representative groups from the peoples, tribes, tongues, and races will gaze upon their corpses for three and a half days, nor will they allow their corpses to be placed in a tomb for that period. Earth's denizens, moreover, will rejoice over them and make merry — they will even send gifts of joy to one another — because these two prophets had really distressed earth's peoples.

But three days and a half afterward the Spirit of Life which issues from God entered them and they stood upon their feet. Then great fear fell upon those who were watching them. And they heard a mighty voice saying out of heaven to them, "Come up here."

So as their enemies looked on, they ascended into heaven in a cloud. At that very hour a terrific earthquake occurred and a tenth part of the city fell in ruins. The count of the people killed by the earthquake numbered seven thousand. Moreover, the rest becoming terrified gave praise to the God of heaven.

The second Woe has passed. Look — the third Woe will occur forthwith. (11:1–14)

THE PERSECUTION of the Church — whose mention John would have avoided — at once begins! God saves his people, however, though not " out of " trial and sorrow, rather " in the midst of " them by granting them a spirit of fortitude and faith such as others cannot receive (John 14:27; 16:33; 17:15).

This thought is expressed here by the command to the seer to *measure* the *sanctuary,* as well as *those who* at the opening of this act we saw assembled there to *worship.* To *measure,* in the language of apocalyptic, has the same significance as the sealing which took place in Scene 6 of Act II — namely, to protect or save (Ezek. 40; Zech. 2:1 ff.).

That God's people, however, are not to be spared from (or, " out of ") the Great Tribulation (7:14) is made plain by the incident here of the *two witnesses.* These represent the witnessing Church and are taken from Zech. 4:2 ff. — they are *two olive trees* or *lampstands* and so full of that oil of God's Spirit which as it burns gives forth the light of the gospel. Their *witnessing* is to occur in *the courtyard outside the sanctuary* or in the *Great City (Sodom, Egypt, that city in which their Lord was crucified)* — that is, in the secular world inhabited by *the nations* which have been won over to the side of *the Beast* by the means described under the symbols of *locusts* (corporate sin) and *horsemen* (secular power) in Woes I and II.

This preaching of the gospel and its attendant trials will last only for the brief time set by God himself (*forty-two months, three and a half days* — see Dan. 7:25). It will be accompanied by " signs " like those attesting the older prophets, Moses and Elijah (*fire* — II Kings 1:10; lack of *rain* — I Kings 17:1; *blood* — Ex. 12:13). At its close, the witnessing Church — like Elijah and its Lord himself (II Kings 2:11; Acts 1:9) — will *ascend into heaven.*

## WORSHIP IN HEAVEN

The seventh angel blew. Then there occurred loud voices in heaven making

### An Announcement

" The Kingdom of the world has passed over
To our Lord and his Messiah,
And he shall reign forever and ever."

Then the twenty-four elders who occupy seats in the Presence of God fell down on their faces and worshiped God, declaring

### Praise of God's Rule

" We give thanks to thee,
Lord God Almighty,
Thou who art and wast,
That thou hast taken up thy great power
And hast begun to reign.
The nations have been enraged,
And thy wrath also has been stirred.
The occasion has arrived for judging the dead
And for rewarding thy servants, the prophets,
The saints also, and those who revere thy name —
Whether small or great —
For destroying, too, those who corrupt the earth."

(11:15–18)

WOES I AND II have left us somewhat aghast — the first with its account of mankind's *torment* achieved by an evil crew out of the *abyss* of hell, the second with that of man's succumbing to the same under the impulse provided by his own passions. Together these two Woes have recounted the sad story of man's resisting the preaching of the gospel message by the Church and of the consequent punishment to be meted out to him on the plane of history — punishment symbolized in Scene 6 by *a terrific earthquake* which takes its toll of human lives.

What, then, remains of human tragedy to be recounted in Woe III? Why, there is still the settling of " the score " for all eternity — thus far we have been speaking only of time and history! There yet remain the account of " Paradise Regained " and that of the " Inferno." We have not spoken even of the " final consummation " of the events of history as yet, not to mention the settlement of man's accounts as these are written down in the Book of Life. Above all, mention must still be made of God's vindication of his righteous rule in earth and heaven.

But to declare all this just now would mean the end of the drama, and as we have seen this must not yet be allowed. The seer must first *prophesy* much more that the gospel may be effectively dramatized (10:11)!

Hence, in Scene 7 we read a mere announcement and hymn of praise — both highly suggestive of these important issues but by no means exhaustively descriptive of them. The end is not yet in sight but our gaze has begun to focus itself in that direction, as our author skillfully effects. Meanwhile, Act III closes as it began, with a picture of the Church at prayer as it faces the thought of persecution in the " last times."

# ACT
# IV

# VISION OF THE CHURCH TRIUMPHANT
## *The Drama of Salvation*
### (Chs. 11:19 to 14:20 and 15:2-4)

*Stage Setting:* The Ark of the Covenant (11:19)

### THE SHOWING OF THE SEVEN PAGEANTS

### (12:1 to 14:20 and 15:2-4)

Scene 1 The Woman and the Dragon (12:1-18)

Scene 2 The Beast Arising from the Sea (13:1-10)

Scene 3 The Beast Arising from the Land (13:11-18)

Scene 4 The Lamb with the 144,000 Martyrs (14:1-5)

Scene 5 The Angel with an Eternal Gospel (14:6-13)
Announcement of the Doom of Babylon

Scene 6 The Son of Man on a White Cloud (14:14-20)
The Wine Press of God's Wrath

Scene 7 The Hymn of the Lamb Chanted by the Saved
(15:2-4)

*Stage Setting: The Ark of the Covenant (11:19)*

(Essentially the same props appear as for Acts II and III. There is, however, sufficient shifting to bring into prominence the whole of the Ark of the Covenant of which the throne is the upper cover or " mercy seat.")

*The seer is speaking as usual —*

The sanctuary of God, which is in heaven, was now wholly opened to view. As a result his Ark of the Covenant which is within the sanctuary became visible. Thereupon occurred lightning, voices, and claps of thunder, together with an earthquake and a violent hailstorm. (11:19)

THOUGH the *sanctuary* has stood open on the stage from Act II forward, this is the first time that it has been shifted into such a prominent position as to be *wholly open to view!* It is not strange that hitherto we have not been able to look with care into this holy place. In olden times none save the current high priest — and he but once a year — was permitted to look upon the *Ark*. It is extraordinary rather that John should permit us to gaze within this sanctuary at all and even more that he should expose it on his cosmic stage! There could be no clearer proof that this is a Christian apocalypse and its sanctuary one Christianly conceived. That all may look within its holy recesses is the seer's way of saying that through the work of Jesus Christ " the veil of the sanctuary has been rent asunder " and there is now " access to the holy place " (Matt. 27:51; Heb. 10:19), and to the mercy seat of God upon the lid of the Ark.

This stage setting exhibits the co-ordination which John would have his readers discern between Acts III and IV. In the former the worshiping Church — expectant of the Great Tribulation — holds the center of the stage. Now, this is set for us to behold God's saving answer to his people's prayers. For Ark and physical phenomena here indicate that his saving purpose will be accomplished.

A word should now be said about the division of Acts IV, VI, and VII into scenes. John does not indicate this in these acts by using groups of seven (letters, seals, trumpets, bowls). Rather, here he opens each scene with the simple " Then I saw " (or, as in 12:1, with " appeared " and in 21:10 and 22:1, " he showed me "). It is because John's readers have generally failed to note this simple literary device that the sevenfold nature of his drama has so largely escaped observation.

## THE WOMAN AND THE DRAGON

An enormous symbolical figure appeared in the sky. It was a Woman garbed with the sun, with the moon beneath her feet, and a crown of twelve stars upon her head. She was pregnant and cried out with pain, in labor to give birth. Another allegorical figure appeared in the sky also — lo! it was a huge fiery Dragon with seven heads and ten horns. Upon its heads it had seven tiaras. Its tail was sweeping up a third part of the, stars out of the sky — afterward it flung them to earth.

### BIRTH OF THE MESSIAH

The Dragon had taken its stand in front of the Woman who was on the point of giving birth, that when she did so it might devour her child! So she bore a son — a male child destined to shepherd all the nations with an iron rod. And her child was snatched up to God and to his throne. Thereupon the Woman fled away into the " desert " where she had a place ready, prepared by God that there they might care for her throughout a thousand, two hundred, and sixty days. (12:1-6)

ALREADY we have had several hints regarding the Great Tribulation through which God's people alone are destined to
pass unscathed (see Act III, Scene 6). Act IV is a detailed account of the manner of their doing so.

In Scene 1 the narrative begins with a condensed account of
the historical career of our Lord. The two focuses of his earthly
existence receive clear mention — the incarnation (*she bore a
Son — a male child*) and the ascension (the *child was snatched
up to God and to his throne*).

The *Woman* who is *in labor* and who bears the *male child* is
not the Virgin Mary but *an enormous symbolical figure* standing, without doubt, for the " people of God," from among
whom the Messiah comes. She is described in terms suggestive
at once of Joseph's dream concerning the family of Jacob (i.e.,
Israel) — Gen. 37:9 — and also of her universal or cosmic significance (*sun, moon, twelve stars*). That this *Woman* stands
for the continuing " people of God " — of which the Christian
Church from the incarnation forward is the true exemplar — is
shown in the further story of her flight *into the " desert "* and
her nurture there throughout three and a half years — the
length of the period of the Great Tribulation (11:2) — as well
as by the specific statement below that *her progeny* are those
who *keep God's commands and bear witness to Jesus* (12:18).

The most significant single item in the portion of the scene
before us is the certain indication of the chronological scheme
with which the seer is working. The Great Tribulation of the
" last times " begins with the incarnation, the historical career
of Jesus Christ. Accordingly, the short span of this eschatological drama — *the three and a half years* or *a time, two times, and
half a time* of Dan. 7:25 — embraces the entire life span of the
Christian Church from Bethlehem to the end of history!

War, then, started up in heaven — it was Michael and his angels fighting against the Dragon. The Dragon and its angels gave battle but did not prevail. So no place was found for them any more in heaven. As a result the huge Dragon — that ancient Serpent called " Devil " and " Satan," the Deceiver of the whole world of mankind — was flung down to earth, its angels along with it.

Thereafter I heard a loud voice in heaven making

### An Announcement

" Our God's salvation, power, and Lordship have just become actual with the achieving of authority on his Messiah's part. For the accuser of our brothers — he who accused them before our God day and night — has been cast out. It was they who conquered him by reason of the blood of the Lamb and their Word of testimony — when death stalked, they did not love their lives! Wherefore, rejoice, O heavens and you inhabitants of the same! But woe to you, O earth and sea — the Devil has gone down to you in high dudgeon, for he knows that he has but little opportunity left."

(12:7–12)

WAR IN HEAVEN! This is a neat symbolic way of saying that the work of Jesus Christ on the plane of history — just recounted on p. 78 — has eternal significance. Earth's coin passes at "face value" in heaven (Matt. 16:19; John 20:23). The career of our Lord from incarnation to ascension is taken with utter seriousness by the Father — it changes, indeed, the course of history and of eternity as well.

*Michael* is the guardian prince of God's people in the language of apocalyptic (Dan. 10:13.21). Symbolically, therefore, he is assigned to fight the *Dragon,* a familiar figure which is sufficiently well defined and described here and on p. 78 to defy error as to its identity. In reality, however, this battle was waged, not in heaven but on earth, and not by Michael but by Jesus. For this is the story of his temptations and of his exorcising the Devil's *angels* — the "demons" of the Gospels and the *stars* swept down *to earth* by the Dragon's *tail* above (p. 78). Jesus himself treated this series of fights with Beelzebul, "the prince of demons," after his usual fashion with the language of metaphor and parable (Luke 11:14–23).

It is sometimes suggested by students of apocalyptic that this passage and that on p. 78 should be chronologically reversed — the heavenly battle against sin, it is said, took place before that on earth between our Lord and his tempter. But — quite aside from the fact that nothing in John's narrative warrants such reversal — this method of interpretation imposes upon the drama a type of literalness which is completely foreign to it. In point of fact the seer gives no countenance to the idea that either *Michael,* or the *Dragon* actually exist, or that there ever was or will be *war in heaven!* What an utterly preposterous idea, to be sure — if taken literally!

When the Dragon saw that it had been flung down to earth, it began to pursue the Woman who had given birth to the male child. So the two wings of a mighty eagle were granted the Woman that she might fly away into the desert — to her own place of sanctuary — where she is being nourished for " three and a half times " out of the Serpent's sight. The Serpent spit out of its mouth a riverful of water, as it were, after the Woman, that it might cause her to be carried away in its flood. But earth aided the Woman — for earth opened her mouth and drank down the river that the Dragon had spit out of its mouth.

Then the Dragon was genuinely enraged at the Woman and it went out to do battle with the rest of her progeny — those who keep God's commands and bear witness to Jesus. Accordingly, the Dragon took its stand on the sand by the sea. (12:13–18)

THE DRAGON'S FRUSTRATION at his failure to *devour* the Woman's *male child* — or alternately, his defeat at the hand of *Michael* — is devastating. With a mighty "transfer of emotions" he directs his wrath against the *Woman* herself and *the rest of her progeny!* This makes good symbolism and good psychology. But it happens also to represent good history. For this is an account in the language of metaphor of the persecutions suffered by the Church from the earliest days — as narrated in The Acts of the Apostles — to those behind the Iron Curtain in our own day.

This is the second time that reference has been made to the Church's *place of sanctuary* in the *desert* (12:6). No doubt the original event which forms the pattern for the seer's vision here is Israel's passing of the Red Sea (Ex. 19:4), when Yahweh "bore" his people "on eagle's wings" away from Egypt and the *earth drank down* the *flood* that they might proceed into the *sanctuary* of the *desert*.

The wider reference of this symbolic language will be to the *sanctuary* provided to the Christian community by its Lord down the short stretch of history. In this secure spot it is always *being nourished* "in green pastures" and "beside still waters" by the Great Shepherd who refuses to allow one of his sheep to perish (Ps. 23). Such refuge for God's people will last down the short epoch to the end of history — the *three and a half times* of John's vision and of apocalyptic generally, and the equivalent of half the symbol for eternity's perfect time (seven).

That *the Dragon took its stand on the sand by the sea* leads us to the next episode in the drama. The might of the Roman Empire was sprawled on the shores about the Mediterranean Sea in John's day. To him and his compatriots in the Christian Church "the might of Rome" was the veritable incarnation of Satan's strength and Rome's inland *sea* a neat symbol of the *pit of the abyss*.

# THE BEAST ARISING FROM THE SEA

I next saw a Beast coming up out of the sea. It had ten horns and seven heads. On its horns were ten coronets and upon its heads, blasphemous names inscribed. This Beast which I beheld was like a leopard generally but its feet resembled those of a bear, and its mouth, that of a lion.

Now, the Dragon committed its power, its throne, and great authority to this Beast. One of its heads appeared as though stabbed to death, but its death wound had been healed. The whole earth was wonder-struck at the Beast — they worshiped the Dragon because it gave its authority to the Beast. They worshiped the Beast as well, saying: "Who can compare with this Beast? Who can join battle with it?"

So the Beast was conceded "a mouth speaking big things" — blasphemies they were, indeed — it was allotted a certain authority too, to carry on for forty-two months. Whenever it opened its mouth, it was only to blaspheme God, cursing his name, his dwelling place, and the inhabitants of heaven.

The Beast was permitted to do battle with the saints and to overcome them — in fact, it was granted authority over every tribe, people, tongue, and nation. All earth's denizens, accordingly, will worship it — that is, those whose names are not found written in the Book of the Life of the Lamb that was slaughtered from the world's founding.

If anyone has an ear, let him hearken. "If anyone is meant for captivity, into captivity he goes! If anyone is to be slain by the sword, by the sword he shall be slain!" It is in such circumstances that the steadfastness and faith of the saints become evident. (13:1-10)

Scene I closed with a view of the *Dragon* standing *by the sea*. Scene 2 opens with a vision of *a Beast coming up* out of the same — it bears the likeness of the Dragon whose wish for a living replica of itself to dwell on earth and serve as its Messiah has evidently brought forth this Beast from the depths. The similarity between the two figures is intentional — each has *ten horns* representing power and *seven heads* signifying the totality of the "underworld's" wisdom and understanding.

John has already employed this *Beast* at 11:7, where it is described as coming *up from the abyss* to engage the witnessing Church *in battle* — further proof that Act IV is an elaboration of the events there described and so of the Great Tribulation generally.

There can be no doubt that this *Beast,* the Dragon's messiah, stands for the secular world culture generally. To begin with, it is described in terms of the creaturely characteristics which in Dan. 7:4 ff. represent the kingdoms of the world. Then, it wears *ten coronets* — the mark of dominion — and its heads are *inscribed* with *blasphemous names* indicative of its opposition to the living God. That the Dragon has *committed* its *authority* to the Beast means that the world culture has become Satan's messiah and is dedicated to bringing about his rule in the affairs of men — hence man's *worshiping* of both figures. In John's day the Roman emperor embodied in his person these attributes of the Beast.

The Beast has only *a certain authority,* however, and for no longer than suits God's plan — viz., the *forty-two months* of the period of the Great Tribulation or the "last times." During this time the lines will be clearly drawn between the *saints* of God and those who serve the Beast. The quotation in the last paragraph is from Jer. 15:2, where God's disgust with rebellious man is further recorded in the words, "Send them out of my sight, and let them go!"

## Scene 3
## THE BEAST ARISING FROM THE LAND

Then I saw another Beast — this one arising from the land. It had two horns similar to those of a lamb but it spoke like a dragon.

This Beast exercised all the authority of the first Beast in its sight. It caused earth and its denizens to worship the first Beast — the one particularly whose death wound had been healed. Indeed, it performed great miracles — for example, it caused fire to descend out of the sky onto the ground in the sight of mankind. It led astray the denizens of earth by reason of these miracles which it was permitted to perform in sight of the first Beast. It even persuaded earth's inhabitants to make an image of that Beast that had suffered the sword stroke and lived through it.

Then it was granted power to give breath to the image of the other Beast — with the result that that Beast's image spoke. Moreover, it caused all to be slain who refused to worship the Beast's image.

Also it made everyone — both small and great, rich and poor, freemen and slaves — to be branded with a mark on either the right hand or the forehead. This was done with a view to none being able to buy or sell unless he possessed the mark — either the name of the Beast or the number signifying his name! And here Wisdom is with us — let anyone having a mind for it, reckon the number of the Beast, for it is a certain man's number — and its number is " six hundred, sixty-six." (13:11–18)

A NOTHER *Beast* — this time *from the land!* In the seer's vision Satan is duplicating point for point the entire organization of God's Kingdom on earth. Scene 2 disclosed the Dragon's messiah — the secular world culture dominant at any period in world history. Here in Scene 3 we are shown the cult or religious institution designed to give secular culture a religious sanction in men's minds. It apes the power (the *two horns*) of the Lamb (5:6), and as the latter was *slaughtered* so it has a *death wound* (5:6), but it speaks *like a dragon* — "a wolf in sheep's clothing," indeed!

This *Beast arising from the land* in John's day took the form of emperor worship whose "god" was the continuing line of Roman emperors deified by decree of the Roman Senate. This cult had behind it *the authority* of the emperor (*the first Beast*) — in the name of that authority it exercised (*a*) the priestly office of leading men *to worship* the emperor's *image,* (*b*) the prophetic function of performing *great miracles* to validate the State religion, and (*c*) the power of Grand Inquisitor, branding all men *with a mark* (reminiscent of the *seal* on the foreheads of God's people — 7:1–8), without which no one was *able to buy or sell* — a prohibition intended in a totalitarian State to spell slow death by starvation.

Here and in Scene 2 reference is made to the Beast's *head* which appeared to be *stabbed to death* though its *death wound had been healed*. There can be no doubt that Nero is intended. As in the case of other tyrants, rumor had it that he had been stabbed and fled to the East to return again, or alternatively that, though he had died, he would rise again more monstrous than before (as *Nero redivivus*). Again, the number *666* is best explained as the sum of the numerical values of the Hebrew letters spelling "Neron Caesar" — thus, נ–50, ר–200, ו–6, ן–50; ק–100, ס–60, and ר–200.

## THE LAMB WITH THE 144,000 MARTYRS

Again I saw a sight — lo! the Lamb was standing on Mount Zion and with him a hundred, forty-four thousand who had his name and his Father's name written upon their foreheads. Moreover, I heard a sound issuing from heaven — like that of many waters or of loud thunder it was — indeed, the sound that I heard was like that of harpers playing their harps. They were singing a new hymn before the throne and in front of the four creatures and the elders. No one, moreover, was able to learn the hymn except the hundred and forty-four thousand who had been purchased from the earth.

These are they who have never been defiled by women — they are " virgins." They are the Lamb's followers, going along with him wherever he goes. They have been purchased from among mankind. A " first fruits " they are for God and the Lamb — in their mouth no lie has been discovered — they are " without blemish." (14:1–5)

IT IS SIGNIFICANT that Scene 4 follows at once upon the dismal picture at which we have been looking in Scene 3. A contrast of the most absolute sort is here intended. It is the total number of those who have the *seal* of *the Lamb* and of *his Father's name* over against the like group wearing *the mark of the Beast*. We have already met this *hundred, forty-four thousand* (p. 52), and we have noted that they are one with the *huge multitude which no one was able to count* out of *every race* (p. 54) — the martyred Church of Christ in its entirety.

This multitude of the saved, as in the latter context, are *singing a new hymn* known only to those *purchased* by the *Lamb*. They wear the court dress which gives them access to *the throne* — the *white flowing robe* of sanctity — for they *have never been defiled*. The phrase *by women* is no doubt an unconscious slip on John's part — for both martyrs and Church include women! — perhaps due to "virgins" in Greek being masculine in form though commonly used to refer to both sexes.

For Israel's psalmists and prophets *Mount Zion* was the symbol for the certainty of God's saving purpose (Ps. 125:1), as well as the rallying ground for "all the nations . . . and . . . peoples" whose intent was to serve the living God (Isa. 2:2 ff.; Hos. 4:1 ff.). Moreover, Zion was to become the center of the gospel's proclamation (Isa. 52:7 ff.; Acts 10:36), even as it had once been that of the dissemination of the Law (Isa. 2:3). Accordingly, the *sound issuing from heaven* and the *new hymn* which forms its content will be the gospel in process of being proclaimed by *the Lamb's followers* (see the co-ordinate passages on p. 54 and again in Act VI, Scene 4 on p. 128; also Matt. 10:7). There is nothing incongruous about this suggestion that the "good news" is sung as a hymn — indeed, it has been so since the inception of the Christian movement!

# THE ANGEL WITH AN ETERNAL GOSPEL

## Announcement of the Doom of Babylon

Then I beheld an angel flying in midheaven. He had an " eternal gospel " to proclaim to those dwelling on earth, even to every nation, tribe, tongue, and people. He uttered it with a mighty voice, shouting out: " Revere God and give him praise, for the hour of his judgment has arrived. Worship him who created heaven and earth, sea and the water springs."

Another angel too, a second one, followed, crying —

### An Announcement

" Fallen! Fallen is Babylon the Mighty — she that caused all the nations to drink of the wine of the wrath of her fornication."

Another angel also, a third one, followed these, shouting out with a loud voice —

### A Second Announcement

" If anyone worships the Beast and its image, if anyone accepts its mark upon either forehead or hand, he shall also drink of the wine of God's wrath — wine which, mixed in the cup of his wrath, maintains its pure strength! — he shall be tormented with fire and brimstone in the presence of both the holy angels and the Lamb. Moreover, the smoke of their torment shall ascend for endless ages and they shall find no rest day or night — such is the lot of those who worship the Beast and its image, who receive the mark bearing its name! "

In such a situation the steadfastness of the saints — of those who keep the commands of God and their faith in Jesus — becomes apparent. So I heard a voice from heaven declaring, " Write this — ' Blessed are the dead who die in the Lord.' " " From now on," says the Spirit, " they will rest from their labors. For their works accompany them."

(14:6–13)

Scene 5 is intended to be by way of appeal to the peoples of the world to join the forces of righteousness and of comfort to the martyred Church — God is about to receive them into his *rest* (Heb. 4:10). In Scenes 3 and 4 we have had a glimpse of the two hosts preparing for the final conflict — those with *the mark of the Beast* representative of the secular world culture and those with the *seal* of *the Lamb,* the community of Christian believers. Now, just before that conflict begins, three closely related announcements intended to produce a single effect are rapidly made.

The first of these contains an appeal to all peoples *dwelling on earth* to *revere God,* the Creator and Judge — this is the "gospel of the Kingdom" of Jesus' own preaching ministry (Matt. 4:23). The second pronounces impending doom on *Babylon the Mighty,* or the world empires of Scene 3. The third is a warning to those who persist in *worshiping* the *Beast* that *torment* for *endless ages* awaits them. All these declarations represent various aspects of the gospel message — some negative, some positive.

The over-all motivation of Act IV becomes very clear at this point — it is to commend the *saints* for their steadfastness and comfort them in the dire *situation* awaiting them in the Great Tribulation. They will *die in the Lord,* so finding *rest* with him, and the effect of *their works* will accompany them into heaven and be registered there.

This is the first time that the seer has termed the "City of Vanity Fair" *Babylon the Mighty.* Elsewhere he has spoken of the *Holy City* (11:2), *Sodom* and *Egypt,* or the *Great City . . . in which their Lord was crucified* (11:8). It is all one by whatever name she be called — she is also Rome, Calcutta, London, New York — anywhere and everywhere that men worship something other than the true and living God.

# THE SON OF MAN ON A WHITE CLOUD

## The Wine Press of God's Wrath

Another spectacle! — it was a white cloud and upon the cloud a seated figure — likeness of the " Son of Man "! On his head he had a golden crown, and in his hand a sharp sickle.

Now there issued from the sanctuary a first angel shouting in a loud voice to him who was seated on the cloud: " Thrust in your sickle and reap. For the hour for reaping has come — earth's harvest is ripe! " So the figure seated on the cloud thrust his sickle on the earth and it was reaped.

Again, a second angel issued from heaven's sanctuary. He too held a sharp sickle. Then, from the direction of the altar of sacrifice came a third angel who had authority over fire. He too shouted with a mighty voice to the other who held the sharp sickle: " Thrust in your sharp sickle and gather the clusters of earth's vineyard. For its grapes have ripened." So the angel thrust in his sickle on the earth and reaped earth's vineyard. Then he threw the clusters into the great winevat of God's wrath. The winevat was trodden outside the city and blood flowed out of it up to the bridles of horses in depth and a thousand, six hundred stadia in extent. (14:14–20)

A ND NOW the final issue between the causes of good and evil is graphically portrayed in the imagery of the harvest field. The parallel Scene 6 in Acts III, V, and VI describes this same event in terms of battle in some part. In the present act, however — where the emphasis lies upon the Church's salvation in the Tribulation of the last times — the symbol of the harvest exhibits how clearly the issues of life are in the hands of God. He needs only to *thrust in* his *sickle and reap!*

Like Scene 6 of Act III, the source of this incident appears to be The Book of Joel — the prophet's third chapter is devoted to a scene combining the features of warfare and judgment under the imagery of harvest. In the Valley of Jehoshaphat near Jerusalem " all . . . nations . . . gather themselves," while the Lord also " bring[s] down . . . warriors " to meet them — and here he will " sit to judge all the nations round about " (vs.11 f.). At this point the prophet reports the significant command —

> " Put in the sickle,
>     for the harvest is ripe.
> Go in, tread,
>     for the wine press is full.
> The vats overflow,
>     for their wickedness is great." (v.13)

This is a picture of judgment with its two sides of salvation and condemnation — *reaping* standing for the first, *treading* the *winevat* for the second — or so John appears to treat the matter whether Joel does or not. Our Lord used *harvest* as a symbol of the garnering in of the saved (Mark 4:29; Luke 10:2) — and significantly the *Son of Man* in this scene is concerned only with this saving aspect of the Judgment — he *thrust his sickle on the earth and it was reaped*. The picture of wine flowing from the vat lends itself, contrariwise, as an apt symbol for the sentence of condemnation and its effect in the pouring out of the culprit's lifeblood!

## THE HYMN OF THE LAMB CHANTED BY THE SAVED

Then I beheld, as it were, a glassy sea in which fire was mixed. Standing by this glassy sea were those who had come off victors from their encounters with the Beast and its image and with him whose name is indicated by the number. They had God's harps and were singing the Hymn of Moses, God's servant, and the Hymn of the Lamb, thus —

### Hymn of the Redeemed

" Great and marvelous are thy deeds,
O Lord God Almighty,
Righteous and faithful are thy ways,
Thou King of the nations!

Who will not revere thee, O Lord,
and glorify thy name?
For thou only art holy,
All nations will come
and worship before thee,
For thy righteous deeds are manifest! "

(15:2–4)

THIS LAST SCENE of Act IV depicts in a few bold strokes the end of history for the *victors* in life's warfare. The seer here brings to a fitting conclusion the theme with which he has been dealing in Acts III and IV. His purpose has been to recount the events of the last times — hitting only the "high spots," to be sure — as these affect the community of believers, Christ's redeemed people.

Accordingly, in Scene 7 we see only this saved group *standing by* the *glassy sea*. They have passed through it, even as Israel did through the Red Sea. The *fire* of its judgment has served merely to purify — not to destroy — them. So like Israel they pause to sing the *Hymn of Moses* (Ex. 15:1 ff.), with such necessary modifications of the original as will serve to make it also the *Hymn of the Lamb*.

The term *glassy sea* is reminiscent of the name given to the ten huge lavers of Solomon's Temple and the *molten sea* that went with them (I Kings 7:23-39). Like these, it stands for the sanctity without which man cannot approach God. The redeemed here are pictured as having passed through its depths and standing on the shore nearer the throne. They sing and play upon *God's harps* in proof that for them the purpose of true religion has been achieved — namely, ready and constant access to and fellowship with God on man's part (Heb. 10:19 ff.). They have now "confidence to enter the sanctuary" and to *worship before* God because his *righteous deeds* from the day of *Moses* to that of the *Lamb* have given them that "assurance of faith" which men require to "draw near" to the true and living God.

So the curtain falls on Act IV, leaving us with the confident assurance that those who have God's seal on their foreheads need never fear the Tribulation of the last times!

# Act V

## VISION OF THE SEVEN ANGELS OF GOD'S WRATH

### *The World in Agony*

(Chs. 15:1, 5 to 16:21)

*Stage Setting:* The Sanctuary of the "Tabernacle of Testimony" (15:1, 5–8; 16:1)

#### THE POURING OUT OF THE SEVEN BOWLS (16:2–21)

Scene 1   The Plague to the Earth: Boils on Men (16:2)

Scene 2   The Plague to the Sea: Blood (16:3)

Scene 3   The Plague to Rivers and Springs: Blood (16:4–7)

Scene 4   The Plague to the Sun: Burning Heat (16:8, 9)

Scene 5   The Plague to the Beast's Throne: Darkness (16:10, 11)

Scene 6   The Plague to the Euphrates: Drying Up (16:12–16)
Gathering at Armageddon

Scene 7   The Plague to the Air: Devastation (16:17–21)
Announcement of the Destruction of Babylon

*Stage Setting: The Sanctuary of the " Tabernacle of Testimony " (15:1, 5–8; 16:1)*

(In this act the sanctuary is shifted to the rear so as to be seen with all its " saving features " (lampstands, altars, etc.) in perspective and as it were as distant background. More prominently displayed are the seven angels with the seven bowls of God's wrath issuing from the door of the sanctuary.)

*The narrator is speaking —*

After this I beheld another symbolic figure in the sky — greatly stirring it was — seven angels with the seven last plagues, last because with them God's wrath is brought to final fruition.

Now, as I looked, the sanctuary of the tabernacle of testimony opened in heaven and from the sanctuary issued forth the seven angels who have the aforementioned seven plagues. They were garbed in pure, shining linen and girded about the chest with golden girdles.

One of the four creatures had given these seven angels seven bowls of gold brimful of the wrath of God who lives forever and ever. Then the sanctuary filled with smoke by reason of God's glory and power. So no one was able to enter the sanctuary until the accomplishment of the seven plagues now in the seven angels' hands.

Then I heard a loud voice proceeding from the sanctuary and thus addressing the seven angels: " Go. Pour out the seven bowls of God's wrath upon earth." (15:1, 5–8; 16:1)

ACT V is in contrast to Act III. In Act III we saw the Church in the Great Tribulation of the last times. Now we are to observe the secular world under the same conditions. Accordingly the present act is the shortest of the drama — a mere sketch intended to underline the difference between two attitudes toward the same events. There is a marked contrast between the two acts as regards the figures who do God's bidding — in the one, *the seven angels of the Presence,* symbols of God's saving power; in the other, *the seven angels with the seven last plagues* garbed as priests, through whom *God's wrath* is effected.

The source of John's motif here is without doubt Lev. 26:2, where dire warning of *God's wrath* toward Israel for her disobedience is given in the words, " If you walk contrary to me, and will not hearken to me, I will bring every plague upon you, sevenfold as many as your sins." The use of *seven* fits nicely John's use of that number — as there is a sevenfold revelation of God's saving power, so there ought to be a sevenfold exhibition of his wrath against man's sin.

There is further contrast here with Acts III and IV as regards approach to the *sanctuary.* In those acts we saw the Church at prayer and the Ark of the Covenant fully displayed. Here the sanctuary is pushed into the background and *no one is able to enter* it until *God's wrath* is expended! This thought is taken from Ex. 40:34 ff. — there " Moses was not able to enter the tent of meeting, because . . . the glory of the Lord filled " it, that is to say, because for the moment the majesty of God's Presence was too overpowering for man to look upon. Here this will mean that nothing can stay *God's wrath* against a sinful world — approach to him is closed and there is no recourse for disobedient men during the period of the Great Tribulation. Little wonder that the act closes with the words, " The distress . . . was exceedingly devastating."

## Scene 1

### THE PLAGUE TO THE EARTH: *Boils on Men*

So the first angel went away and poured out his bowl onto the earth. A pernicious and painful sort of ulcer as a result attacked those humans who had on them the mark of the Beast and who worshiped its image. (16:2)

## Scene 2

### THE PLAGUE TO THE SEA: *Blood*

Then the second angel emptied his bowl into the sea. And it turned, so to speak, into corpse's blood. So every sort of sea life died. (16:3)

## Scene 3

### THE PLAGUE TO RIVERS AND SPRINGS: *Blood*

Again, the third angel poured out his bowl into the rivers and water springs. This too produced blood. So I heard the angel of the waters asserting: "Righteous art thou who art and wast, O Holy One. For this is thy judgment that, whereas men have poured out the blood of saints and prophets, thou hast given them blood to drink! — Well, they deserved it."

Then I heard a voice from the altar of sacrifice saying, "Yea, O Lord God Almighty, faithful and righteous are thy decisions." (16:4–7)

## Scene 4

### THE PLAGUE TO THE SUN: *Burning Heat*

Then the fourth angel emptied his bowl into the sun. And it was allowed to scorch mankind with its fire. So when people began to be burned with the terrific heat, they started blaspheming the name of God who has authority over these plagues. Nor did they repent and give him praise. (16:8, 9)

THE FOUR SCENES on the opposite page are in exact duplication of the corresponding ones in Act III. The same order of catastrophies is observed in each series. Moreover, as both series contain an elaboration of the cosmic catastrophies summarily presented in Scene 6 of Act II, this clearly places the events of Acts III and V in the period of the last times.

There is just one difference — and that a significant one — in the account of these events in Acts III and V. This concerns the extent to which the tribulations of these scenes are said to affect mankind. In Act III, it is only at Scene 3 that man is said to suffer from them. This is because John's purpose there is to deal with the Church and to show how it will successfully weather the gale of those troublous times. Here, on the contrary, in every scene stress is laid on the effect of these plagues on men who have *on them the mark of the Beast and who worship its image.* And that effect is clear — ungodly men will not be ready to meet the vicissitudes of those days and in the endeavor to cover up their own inadequacies they will *start blaspheming the name of God who has authority over these plagues.*

Act V, accordingly, presents a picture of human suffering which rises in a crescendo. In Scene 1 *pernicious ulcers* attack rebellious man (Ex. 9:10 ff.). These result in widespread fatalities — so much so that *corpses* are flung into the *sea* (Scene 2), a scene reminiscent of the last plague at the Exodus in Egypt (Ex. 11:4 ff.). Even *the rivers and water springs* are eventually contaminated (Scene 3), and men have only *blood to drink* — a fate they have richly *deserved* (Ex. 7:19 f.). While in this agony of thirst, the sun is *allowed to scorch* God's enemies *with its fire* (Scene 4).

What a picture of unrelieved torment! This exhibition of God's wrath against sin is the gospel message in reverse.

## SCENE 5

## THE PLAGUE TO THE BEAST'S THRONE: *Darkness*

Now the fifth angel poured out his bowl upon the Beast's throne. This resulted in its kingdom being darkened — so intense it was that men gnawed their tongues in distress. They even blasphemed the God of heaven by reason of their pains and sores. Nor did they repent from their ways. (16:10, 11)

A ND NOW the attack is carried forward to the very citadel of the Beast! Its *kingdom* is *darkened*. It is a darkness that can be felt — more, it is so intense as to cause great *distress* to those who at every turn of affairs are prepared to *blaspheme the God of heaven* for the ills that befall them. These are clearly to be identified with the men who *had on them the mark of the Beast* in Scene 1.

In Scripture "light" is the symbol of God's eternal truth which brings life and salvation to man (Isa. 9:2; John 1:4); *darkness* symbolizes its opposite — falsehood and man's destruction (Rom. 1:21 ff.). Comparison of the relevant passages in Acts IV and VI suggests that the great battle in the last times which John wishes to record is one between ideologies and not one of swords and guns (see particularly pp. 89 and 129). The Beast's followers are engaged in a type of propaganda on behalf of Satan's rule that may rightly be termed a "badspel" to distinguish it from the "gospel" of light and truth. Accordingly, the punishment which they are made to suffer is advisedly to "eat their own words" — or, to use the seer's expressive phrase, to *gnaw their tongues in distress!* Satan's badspel "backfires," so to speak, in a world which belongs to God and not to him.

The eighth and ninth plagues at the Exodus from Egypt were respectively *locusts* (Ex. 10:3 ff.) and *darkness* (vs.21 ff.). Perhaps it was this fact that suggested to John the use of the same two plagues in that order respectively at the fifth scene in Acts III and V. In the former of these, Apollyon was seen leading up his forces like a huge swarm out of *the pit of the abyss* to attack mankind. Both there with the *locusts* and here with the *darkness* it is clear that only men who yield themselves to Apollyon's leadership can in the end be hurt in God's world.

## THE PLAGUE TO THE EUPHRATES: *Drying Up*

### Gathering at Armageddon

Next, the sixth angel poured forth his bowl upon the mighty river Euphrates. So its water dried up in preparation for a highway over which the kings from the east might travel. Then I beheld three unclean spirits resembling frogs springing out of the mouths of the Dragon, the Beast, and the false prophet. Now, these are miracle-working demonic spirits that are to go forth into the domains of the kings of all the world with a view to gathering them for battle on the great " Day of God Almighty."

(*In the background a voice is heard saying* —

(" Lo! I am coming as a thief. Blessed is he who stays awake and keeps his clothing handy, lest he be found walking around naked and people observe his nakedness.")

So he brought them together at the place called in Hebrew " Armageddon." (16:12–16)

THAT THIS SCENE is the duplicate of Scene 6 in Act III surely needs no argument. In both the *Euphrates* is significantly mentioned and in both a mighty marching host is suggested — here led by *the kings from the east* and requiring the *preparation* of a special highway for its accommodation. This is the powerful array of the world culture opposed to God's rule over mankind (p. 67).

It is high time that remark be made — in more comprehensive fashion than hitherto — of the nature of the Battle of *Armageddon*. This is its first mention by name in the seer's drama, though we have hints of its coming in Scene 6 of Acts III and IV (see also p. 103 and later in Act VI, p. 132). Contrary to every theory involving a literal interpretation of this book, it should be clear that this is a battle of opposing cultures waged by opposing ideologies. Here this point is made under the symbolism of *three unclean spirits . . . springing out of the mouths of the Dragon, the Beast, and the false prophet.* Apocalyptic is unable to confront us with a clearer picture of lying propaganda than this! Its function is — as is true of all such proclamation of the badspel — the *gathering* of men who bear the mark of the Beast for the moral battle against God's forces of righteousness.

This is again the "V *Day*" of God Almighty (p. 53) proclaimed by the Hebrew prophets from the time of Amos onward (Amos 5:18). As Amos declared, it is a day of "darkness, and not light." Hence, in an aside the Lord interjects that he is *coming as a thief* — for thieves come in the *darkness!* — for his share in this battle of ideologies (Matt. 24:43). That the *unclean spirits resemble frogs* is probably an allusion to the second plague at the Exodus (Ex. 8:2 ff.) and the drying up of the *Euphrates* suggests that of the Red Sea, but in reverse — for the forces of evil rather than those of righteousness, and to hasten the battle, not delay it.

## THE PLAGUE TO THE AIR: *Devastation*

### ANNOUNCEMENT OF THE DESTRUCTION OF BABYLON

Lastly, the seventh angel emptied his bowl into the air. And there issued from the throne within the sanctuary a mighty shout, declaring, "It is accomplished." This was followed by lightning flashes, noises, and claps of thunder. And there occurred an earthquake of such dimensions that its like had never previously been known since mankind began to live on the earth — it was just that severe.

The Great City was split into three parts and the cities of the nations fell. Then was Babylon the Mighty called to remembrance in the Presence of God that he might give her to drink from the cup of his wrath's hot indignation. So every island disappeared and no mountains remained visible. Enormous quantities of hailstones too — as it were tons in weight — fell from the sky upon mankind and they blasphemed God for this plague of hail, because the distress from it was exceedingly devastating. (16:17–21)

THE SHOUT, "*It is accomplished*," is God's confirmation of the work of the Lamb (5:5 and p. 45). It echoes Jesus' own words to the same effect from the cross (John 19:30). The *earthquake* too is reminiscent of that at the end of the agony on Calvary (Matt. 27:51; Mark 15:38).

Probably the *seventh angel's bowl* is *emptied into the air* in token of the general nature of the effects of this last plague. In Scene 6 of Act III but a *tenth part* of the *Great City* of "Vanity Fair" fell in ruins and a small part only of mankind — some *seven thousand* — failed to be terrified and repent, giving praise to God. Here the implication is that the end has at last fully come — the *Great City, Babylon the Mighty,* symbol of the cultures of *the cities of the nations,* has finally fallen, splitting apart in her fall. Nor is the portrayal of man's blasphemy relieved by the suggestion that any return to his worship. A terrific *earthquake,* an *enormous quantity of hailstones, every island's* and *mountain's* disappearance — these natural catastrophies conspire to paint for us a picture of what can only be the end of the world and its secularism.

This scene of terror is in sharp contrast with its fellow in Act III. There as here we are viewing the end of the series of events constituting the Great Tribulation in the last times. But what a different scene there greets our eyes — it is a picture of the community of believers at worship in heaven, of peace at last established between God and man, of man's salvation and of his consequent praise to God, his Saviour. Here the scene is replete with terror, blasphemy, and devastation.

As the curtain falls on Act V, we can but look forward with trepidation for the filling in of details in the Drama of Judgment which it is Act VI's function to perform!

# Act
## VI

# VISION OF BABYLON'S OVERTHROW
### *The Drama of Judgment*
(Chs. 17:1 to 20:3, 7–10)

*Stage Setting:* One of the Angels of the Seven Plagues Issuing from the Sanctuary (17:1, 2)

THE UNFOLDING OF THE SEVEN PLAGUES (17:3 to 20:3, 7–10)

Scene 1    The Woman on the Scarlet Beast (17:3–5)

Scene 2    The Beast at War with the Woman (17:6–18)

Scene 3    The Final Cosmic Oratorio (18:1 to 19:10)

Scene 4    The Word of God on the White Horse (19:11–16)

Scene 5    The Angel Standing in the Sun (19:17, 18).

Scene 6    The Battle of Armageddon (19:19–21)

Scene 7    Satan Cast Into the Abyss (20:1–3)

Parenthetic Prophecy on His Limited Authority (20:7–10)

*Stage Setting: One of the Angels of the Seven Plagues Issuing from the Sanctuary (17:1, 2)*

(As Act VI follows logically upon Act V, carrying through the same theme essentially, there is no difference in the arrangement of the stage props. One of the angels of the seven plagues is more prominently displayed than the others in view of his having a leading part. But as in Act IV, all the action is conceived as done in sight of the sanctuary.)

*John continues —*

Then there came one of the seven angels who had the seven bowls. He addressed me, saying: " Come here. I shall show you the judgment passed on the Great Harlot who is ensconced over many waters. It is she with whom the kings of earth have been committing fornication and with the wine of whose adultery earth's dwellers have been made drunk."

So he took me away in spirit into a desert. (17:1, 2)

ONE MOTIF runs throughout this act and the last — a phenomenon that we have already observed in the case of Acts III and IV (see p. 63). Little shift in the stage setting, therefore, now occurs. If anything, the sanctuary is pushed farther to the rear of the stage that the wide reaches of earth's farthest outposts may become visible. But the throne of God with the worshiping creatures and elders is yet to be seen in the remote distance, as is clear in Scene 3 (p. 124). After all, *the judgment passed on the Great Harlot* is God's doing, nor may his all-seeing eye fail to observe that judgment executed — and it is this which forms the theme of the present act.

It is characteristic of John's literary technique that occasionally he brings a principal character upon the stage abruptly and without previous introduction or description. This is the case of *the Beast* arising *from the abyss* (p. 70). In the present act the *Great Harlot* is treated in this summary fashion — though the reader may perhaps guess her to be identified with the *Great City* (p. 70), whose *fornication* has been condemned (p. 90), it is not at once said that this is the case. Nor are the *many waters* over which she presides given immediate definition. Following the seer's method, we shall leave more precise statement regarding these matters until the curtain rises on Scenes 1 and 2.

Meanwhile, for the second time *a desert* stretches before us on the stage (p. 78). Nothing could render it more certain that the present act is to treat of the same eschatological situation as that which confronted us in Act IV. The word has an ominous sound. God has, it is true, *prepared* a *place* to *care* for his Church in the desert (p. 78) — but in Scripture generally it has been a place of temptation (Mark 1:12), rebellion (Heb. 3:8), and punishment (v.17).

# THE WOMAN ON THE SCARLET BEAST

I saw a Woman seated on a scarlet Beast. It was covered with blasphemous names and had seven heads and ten horns. The Woman was garbed in royal purple and scarlet and bedecked with golden ornaments, precious stones, and pearls. In her hand she held a cup of gold full of detestable mixes — the impurities of her fornication. Upon her forehead a name was inscribed — it is a symbolic title — *Babylon the Mighty, Mother of the Harlots and of the Abominations of the Earth.* (17:3-5)

THE *Woman* in this scene is without doubt the contrasting double of that other in Act IV who stands as the symbol of the people of God (p. 78). She represents, therefore, the evil community of the Beast — the people who worship at the shrine of that secular culture that opposes God's rule in the world — they *who wear the mark of the Beast* (p. 91). She is bedecked in the finery that the pagan civilizations can bestow and holds in her hand *a cup of gold* symbolizing its profligacy. It is she whose other names are the *Great City, Babylon the Mighty, Mother of the Harlots, Sodom, Egypt,* Jerusalem, Rome; each of these is, to be sure, merely one of her *symbolic titles* — in reality she stands for those in every clime and time who seek to destroy the community of believers in Jesus Christ.

She rides astride a *scarlet Beast* — this latter is obviously to be associated in some sense with the Dragon of Act IV, as the *seven heads and ten horns* possessed by both clearly indicate. This Beast's association with the Dragon and the *blasphemous names* it bears stamp it certainly as the worldly power which undergirds the secular culture approved by men bearing the mark of the Beast. Further assurance of the correctness of this identification is forthcoming in Scene 2.

This act presents us with a series of seven pageants which, at nearly every point, are the opposite of those found in Act IV. The above exemplifies the point. In spite, however, of the similarity existing between the two acts, John's development of his theme sparkles with an originality which never wanes. As Act VI proceeds, the lesson is driven home with relentless zeal that in God's world evil is always self-destructive and in the end only he can prove the Victor.

## THE BEAST AT WAR WITH THE WOMAN

Now I saw that the Woman was getting drunk on the blood of the saints and on that of the witnesses to Jesus. When I observed this, I was greatly perplexed. But the angel said to me: " Why so perplexed? I shall tell you the symbolic meaning of this Woman and of the Beast with the seven heads and ten horns that supports her.

" The Beast which you have seen once lived but is no more alive, but it is about to come back from the abyss — then it will go away to destruction. Earth's inhabitants — those whose names have not stood written in the Book of Life from the world's creation — will be amazed when they see that the Beast successively existed, passed away, and then has returned.

" Here, then, is the explanation by a mind possessing the divine Wisdom. The seven heads stand for seven hills on which the Woman sits. But they also stand for seven kings — of these, five have already fallen, one lives, and the last has not yet arrived. When this last comes on the scene, he is destined to stay only a short time. The Beast which was and is no more is an eighth by count though actually one of the seven previous to him — he it is that goes away to destruction." (17:6–11)

SCENE 2 leaves no doubt as to the identity of the *scarlet Beast* on which the Great Harlot sits. This is the *Beast coming up out of the sea* of the same scene in Act IV, the symbol of every earthly power that sets itself against God's rule in his world. As in the former scene it came *up out of the sea,* so here it is said to *come back from the abyss,* where it had gone for a time.

This description is meant to show Satan's utter lack of originality — his messiah can do no more than imitate God's Messiah at every point. The latter comes in the incarnation (out of heaven), goes away in the ascension (into heaven), and comes again at the Parousia (from heaven). So the former *once lived* (having come up out of the sea), *is no more* (having gone away into the abyss), and *is about to come back from the abyss.*

In John's day this Beast-messiah was represented by the might of Rome — the contemporary world power. This identification is clear from the mention of the *seven hills on which the Woman sits* — Rome was by all accounts situated on seven hills. It is rendered, if possible, even more certain by the mention of the *seven kings,* particularly by that of the one whose experience is said so nearly to parallel that of the true Messiah. This one is *Nero redivivus,* as we have already seen (p. 87). Numerous attempts have been made to equate the other six kings with Roman emperors, but without success. John as usual is here employing a symbolic number to represent the world powers opposed to God. To limit Satan's messianic dynasty to seven Roman emperors is to impose upon John's poetic imagery a literalism which it will not bear. The flexibility of his symbolism appears in the fact that both the Beast itself and one of its *seven heads* may stand in John's thought for Nero.

"Again, the ten horns which you have observed represent ten kings. They have not yet received their dominion, but they will receive authority as kings who are bound in fealty to the Beast — authority in each case for one brief hour. All these kings have one thought only — to place their power and authority at the Beast's command. They will do battle with the Lamb and the Lamb is destined to conquer them. For he is Lord of Lords and King of Kings, and his retainers are all 'called,' 'chosen,' 'faithful.'"

Moreover, the angel said to me, "The waters which you have noted — those where the Harlot is seated — stand for peoples, crowds, nations, and tongues.

"Now, the ten horns which you have seen, together with the Beast itself — all these will come to hate the Harlot. They will render her devastated and naked. They will devour her flesh and will burn her with fire! This is because God has put it into their hearts to perform his plan — and that plan includes their becoming of one mind in turning over their sovereignty to the Beast! This, then, will go on until the Words of God are all consummated.

"So, the Woman whom you beheld stands for the Great City that owns the lordship over earth's kings!" (17:12–18)

W<small>E ARE NOT</small> yet done with the *kings* and the pomp of the world's *dominion!* The *ten horns* and *ten kings* are no doubt borrowed from the description of Daniel's "fourth beast" (Dan. 7:19–27). The latter "made war with the saints, and prevailed over them, until . . . the time came when the saints received the kingdom" (vs.21 f.) — so here the *ten kings* have *authority* each *for one brief hour* and will *do battle with the Lamb,* but he and *his retainers* will conquer them.

With the *seven kings* previously mentioned, we now have seventeen in all. To endeavor to identify these either with Daniel's *ten kings* described with the "fourth beast" (v.24), or with any group of Roman emperors or their satellite "kings" or "governors," is entirely beside the point. This symbolism is the language of poetry, not of prose, and its message is clear to those equipped with spiritual eyes to see and spiritual ears to hear!

The *Harlot is ensconced over many waters* (p. 110) — now interpreted to mean *peoples, crowds, nations, and tongues.* This serves further to identify her with Rome's peoples and to link her with the *Beast coming up out of the sea* in Scene 2 of Act IV. For John and his contemporaries the Empire was co-extensive with the civilized world and so included within its borders all the *peoples* known to them. But the Harlot is also the *Great City,* and hence from age to age not Rome's peoples only, but also those of every other secular power opposed to the Kingdom of God on earth (see p. 91).

In the end, as is inevitable in a world belonging to and ruled by God, *Beast* and *Harlot* — or secular power and its community of folk — are certain to have a "falling out." Satan becomes divided against Satan — this is inevitable in "a moral universe." And the end for every evil power is internal strife, self-destruction, death.

## SCENE 3
# THE FINAL COSMIC ORATORIO

### AN ANNOUNCEMENT OF BABYLON'S OVERTHROW

After this, I beheld another angel coming down out of the sky. He had great weight of authority and the earth was illumined with his splendor. He shouted out with a powerful voice, as he announced —

"Fallen! Fallen is Babylon the Mighty.
  She has become a lair for demons,
  A prison for every unclean spirit,
  A sanctuary for every dirty, hateful bird.
  For of the passionate wine of her fornication
  Have all the nations drunk —
  The kings of earth have committed adultery with her —
  Earth's merchants have grown rich
  By reason of the grossness of her wantonness."

(18:1-3)

### AN APPEAL TO GOD'S PEOPLE REGARDING BABYLON

Then I heard another voice out of heaven appealing —
"Come out of her, O my people,
  Lest you become her accomplices in sin
  And so share her plagues.
  For her sins have become so heaped up together
  As to reach into the sky.
  God, moreover, has made a memorandum
  Of her unrighteous acts.
  Give it to her, as she has given it to others —
  Pile it on doubly after her own fashion —
  Mix the cup with double strength
  That she has mixed for others —
  To the degree that she has bespangled herself and run riot,
  Let her know torture and mourning.
  For in her heart she declared,
  'I am enthroned a queen — I am no widow,
  Nor shall I ever know bereavement.'
  Wherefore, in a single day shall plagues come upon her —
  Death, mourning, famine — and with fire shall she be burned.
  For mighty is the Lord God who has brought her to judgment."

(18:4-8)

SCENE 3 marks the climax of the seer's prophecy regarding the overthrow of all worldly authority and culture opposed to God's rule within history. Its importance is indicated by its length. Thereafter the action is swift and the end speedily reached in four closing scenes.

This scene comprises a single grand oratorio — it is God's "wrath" set to music! And quite appropriately so. For the scene is the exact antithesis to that of the same number in Act IV. There the *Beast arising from the land* symbolized the priesthood of the emperor cultus and the institution of worship which gave a religious sanction to the secular power and its culture. Accordingly, the downfall of that culture and its religious sanction is a theme as worthy of a musical score as any of the prophetic utterances that have given rise to great oratorios. Many of those utterances were replete with God's condemnation of the contemporary life of man.

The oratorio is constructed along the lines of a worship service. It opens with *an announcement* of its general theme. This is followed by *an appeal* to God's people to leave Babylon — a curious opposing appeal to our "call to worship"! Then follows a crescendo in song composed of doom songs and the Hallelujah Chorus, the whole interspersed with the "sermon" — a prophetic bit of emblematic prophecy.

Large portions of this oratorio are in the "blank verse" characteristic of the Hebrew prophets. There is an occasional rhythm observable and the repetition of words and phrases provides a sort of alliterative cadence. Much of the content is taken bodily from the writings of the Hebrew prophets and pieced together in a most ingenious manner. On the opposite page, the first line of the *announcement* is from Isa. 21:9 and that of the *appeal,* from Jer. 51:45.

# A THREEFOLD DOOM SONG ON BABYLON

### a. By the Kings of Earth

Then shall the kings of earth who committed fornication and played the wanton with her wail and be cut up over Babylon. Standing afar off for very fear of her torment, as they watch the smoke of her burning they shall chant —

> "Woe! Woe! O Mighty City,
> O Babylon, Strong City,
> In a single hour has come thy judgment!"

### b. By Earth's Merchants and Traders

Earth's merchants too shall weep and mourn over her. For there is no one left to buy their wares — wares of gold and silver, of precious stones and pearls; of fine linen, royal purple, silk and scarlet; of every sort of aromatic wood, of ivory utensils and those of the most precious woods, of brass, iron, and marble; of spices like cinnamon, amomum, incense, myrrh, and frankincense; of oil, wine, fine wheat flour, and corn; of cattle, sheep, horses, chariots, and slaves; and of the souls of men. The traffickers in these things — they who have enriched themselves on Babylon — shall stand afar off in fear of her torment weeping and mourning, as they declare —

> "Woe! Woe! The Mighty City,
> She who clothed herself in fine linen, regal purple, and scarlet,
> Who bedecked herself with gold and precious stones and pearls,
> In a single hour, she — so rich — has been rendered desolate!"

### c. By Sea Captains and Sailors

Then every sea captain also and everyone who sails anywhere, sailors and all who work the sea, stood and shouted as they watched the smoke of her burning from afar, "Who is like to the Mighty City?" They even cast dust on their heads as they chanted with weeping and mourning —

> "Woe! Woe! The Mighty City,
> Of whose wealth all who have boats at sea enriched themselves,
> In a single hour has she become desolate!"

*A voice* —

"Rejoice over her, O heaven, ye saints, apostles and prophets. For God has accomplished your sentence of condemnation against her."

(18:9–20)

THIS PART of the oratorio is composed of three "doom songs" in the style of the Hebrew prophets. The latter used this kind of composition with telling effect to announce God's judgment on evil men, societies, cities, and peoples. Ezekiel's prophecy of the doom of Tyre is a good example (Ezek., chs. 26 to 28). That doom song, indeed, has provided John with many of his descriptive phrases here — he has merely transferred the earlier prophet's blasts against Tyre to *Babylon*.

Even John's three principal types of mourners — the *kings, merchants,* and *sailors* — are found in Ezekiel's plot (Ezek. 27:27-33). These three — after the fashion of such literary compositions — give expression to three "lamentations" or "dirges" (see Ezek. 26:17 f.; 27:32-36; Amos 6:1, 4). With bitter irony these dirges pronounce *Woe!* on God's enemies.

In the present instance these are chanted by those who have profited most from the advantages afforded by the secular culture symbolized and supported by the Great Harlot. They are now helpless to save her, however, and can only *cast dust on their heads* and *stand afar off, weeping and mourning* — the traditional symbols of repentance (see Ezek. 27:30-34; Joel 2:12 ff.). The sudden nature of God's judgment is stressed in the thrice-repeated phrase *"in a single hour."* It would be difficult to portray more effectively the complete unexpectedness with which this judgment comes to the secular world and its total lack of preparation to meet the same! All classes involved in and supporting this secular culture are like "that wicked servant" whose master comes "on a day when he does not expect him" and whom the latter punishes accordingly (Matt. 24:45-51).

The "voice" advisedly calls for *rejoicing* on the part of all in the Hebrew-Christian tradition who have had a share in the destruction of Babylon and her wicked culture!

Then a powerful angel took up a stone as large as a great millstone and heaved it into the sea, as he declared —

> " So all of a sudden shall Babylon, the Mighty City,
> Be cast away, and she shall never again be seen.
> Nor shall the sound of harpers, minstrels, flute
>         players, and trumpeters
> Ever again be heard in thee.
> Nor shall artisans of any trade
> Ever again be found in thee.
> Nor shall the sound of a millstone
> Ever again be heard in thee.
> Nor shall the light of a lamp
> Ever again shine in thee.
> Nor shall the voice of bride and bridegroom
> Ever again be heard in thee.
> For the ripe fruit of the lust of thy soul
>         has departed from thee.
> All dainties and splendors
>         have perished from thee.
> No longer shall such things
>         be found in thee.
> For thy merchants were earth's nobles;
> By thy sorcery all the nations were led astray;
> In thee was the blood of prophets and saints found;
> Yea, the blood of all who were ever slaughtered
>         on the earth."

(18:21–24)

A ND NOW, the "recitative" or "sermon" of this oratorio-worship service! It is delivered by a *powerful angel* in the form of an "acted parable" or bit of "emblematic prophecy" after the fashion of the Hebrew prophets. Examples of the same literary form are Jeremiah's linen girdle (Jer. 13:1–11), Hosea's adulteress wife (Hos., chs. 1 to 3), and Ezekiel's mimic siege of Jerusalem (Ezek. 4:1–3). The measuring of the sanctuary in John's drama (p. 70) and the sealing of the martyrs (p. 52) are illustrations of the same prophetic symbolism that appears here in *a stone* being *heaved . . . into the sea.*

The sources from which the seer derived his materials for his sermon are without doubt our Lord's judgment that "a millstone" tied about one's neck and his being "cast into the sea" is preferable to the punishment that he will receive who harms "one of these little ones" of his Church (Mark 9:42), as well as Jeremiah's use of much similar language to symbolize the historical Babylon's downfall (Jer. 51:61–64). In all three instances (Jesus' prophecy, Jeremiah's symbolism, and John's recitative), the world's culture and its peoples are seen to be doomed because these have sought to harm God's own people whose protection and eventual salvation are his deep concern.

In this sermon, it should be noted, the two points that receive stress are Babylon's pagan (anti-God) culture by means of which *all the nations were led astray,* and her persecution both of the Church and also of *all* God's creatures *who were ever slaughtered on the earth.* These two points have been signalized again and again throughout the drama. But it is fitting to a degree that they should receive such summary statement in the sermon at this climactic point in the drama. For this sermon is meant, so to speak, as an official pronouncement of God's vindication of his judgment upon every human institution that opposes his righteous rule in his world.

*a. Hymn of Praise for Destruction of the World Culture*

After this I heard the loud sound of what appeared to be a huge
crowd in heaven chanting —

> " Alleluia!
> Salvation and glory and power belong to our God,
> For faithful and righteous are his judgments —
> He has condemned the Great Harlot
> Who has destroyed the earth with her fornication;
> He has made retribution for the blood of his servants
> Slaughtered by her hand."

*b. Three Antiphons*

Again they sang —

> " Alleluia!
> The smoke of her burning will ascend forever and ever."

The twenty-four elders, moreover, with the four creatures, fell down
and worshiped the God who sits on the throne, saying —

> " Amen! Alleluia! "

A voice issued from the throne too, chanting —

> " Praise our God,
> All you, his servants,
> You who revere him,
> Both small and great."

*c. Hymn of the Church Triumphant*

Moreover, I heard, as it were, the voice of a great multitude — a voice
not unlike the sound of many waters or of mighty claps of thunder,
singing —

> " Alleluia!
> The Lord our God, the Almighty, has begun his reign.
> Let us rejoice and be exceedingly glad,
> Let us ascribe him glory.
> For the marriage of the Lamb has come,
> His bride has got herself ready —
> He has seen to it that she is garbed in fine, pure,
>     shining linen,
> For such linen represents the saints' righteous acts."

(19:1–8)

THE HALLELUJAH CHORUS goes back — as much of our Christian hymnody does — to The Psalms or "Book of Praises" of the Second Temple. Psalms 113 to 118 were known as the "Hallel" or "praise" psalms and were sung at the three principal feasts in Jerusalem. But there were other psalms which, like these, began with "Praise the Lord" ("*Alleluia*"), and the general theme of all such was the *salvation* which God had wrought for his people.

Here this theme dominates the first chorus and three antiphons. God's praise is sung by redeemed humanity (the *huge crowd in heaven* and *the twenty-four elders*) and all creation (*the four creatures*) in the context of the overthrow of the *Great Harlot*. This is clearly the "V Day" of God's *retribution* and of the vindication of his righteous rule in the world.

The closing chorus sung by the whole Church Triumphant is rich in suggestiveness. Its first two lines recall Ps. 118:24 — the closing Hallel Psalm — which reads —

> "This is the day which the Lord has made;
> Let us rejoice and be glad in it."

For the seer "the day" referred to is that on which God really *has begun his reign* — that which signalizes the fact that *the marriage of the Lamb has come*. Anyone who takes the trouble to observe the saints as they appear on this cosmic stage — all *garbed in fine, pure, shining linen,* the court dress demanded in the throne room of the King of Kings — may verify the statement that this day has, indeed, arrived. (Luke 13:29 ff.; 14:16 ff.)

From the materials available in this oratorio itself, it is quite impossible to "date" the events it describes. They belong, of course, to the "last times." Their more exact dating depends upon the mutual relations of Act VI and the rest of the drama.

So the angel said to me, " Write this —

*Blessed are they who are called to the marriage supper of the Lamb."*

Moreover, he added — " These words are among God's verities."
So I fell at his feet to give him reverence.
But he said to me: " Look — not that! I am merely your fellow servant
and the comrade of your brothers who hold to the witness concerning
Jesus. Worship God, then."
(Indeed, this witness to Jesus is the very life breath of prophecy.)

(19:9, 10)

THIS CLOSING EPISODE of Scene 3 is a bit of byplay like that in Act III, Scene 6 — as there, so here John is drawn into the spotlight. We are treated to a bit of the sort of conversation that goes on between the producer (the *angel*) and the narrator (the *seer*) as the drama unfolds. The producer is so eminently satisfied with his cosmic oratorio that he cannot refrain from commenting on its overpowering character. In Handel's *Messiah* the Hallelujah Chorus has from its first performance brought the audience to its feet, a tribute at once to its central Figure and the majesty of its music. Little wonder that the last strains of the present oratorio with their reference to *the marriage supper of the Lamb* should bring the familiar Hebrew ejaculation, *Blessed,* to the angel's lips!

*God's verities* is a meaningful expression with a long history behind it in the Hebrew tradition. It refers to the faithful character of the Bible's God and his faithfulness in fulfilling his promises of salvation to his people. It is his understanding of this overpowering fact that brings John to his knees in *reverence.*

But at this point the consistent theism of the Hebrew prophetic-Christian tradition asserts itself. No creature in that tradition dares presume to share divine honors with the true and living God. There is no room for saint- or angel-worship in the religion of the Scriptures (see also 22:8 f.).

The last sentence may be a parenthetical remark of the seer, though it is equally possible that it is intended as a part of the angel's words. In either case, it again lays stress on the prophetic nature of this apocalypse — a fact that sets it apart from all others of its class (see p. 11). It indicates clearly that for the Church the gospel — or *witness to Jesus* — is the very center of the message of *prophecy.*

## THE WORD OF GOD ON THE WHITE HORSE

Then I beheld heaven standing open. Lo! there is a white horse. He who sits upon it is called " Faithful " and " True " — with righteousness he judges and gives battle. His eyes are a fiery flame — upon his head are many diadems — he has a name written thereon which no one but himself knows — he is garbed in a mantle dyed with blood. His name is given out as " *The Word of God.*"

His retinue follow him in heaven upon white horses and are clothed in fine, white, clean linen.

Out of his mouth proceeds a sharp sword that therewith he may smite the nations. Indeed, he shall shepherd them with an iron staff — he shall tread the wine press of the fury of the wrath of God Almighty. He has on his mantle and on his thigh this title inscribed — " *King of Kings and Lord of Lords.*" (19:11–16)

ANOTHER RIDER on a *white horse!* This one, however, is the antithesis of the other in the drama — the first of the Four Horsemen of Act II. For he comes forth from *heaven,* which is now *standing open,* in other words from the sanctuary at the back of the stage. *No one . . . knows* his *name* in full — to do so, in Semitic circles, would mean to fathom to the depth of his Person, to discover the last " mystery " of the being of God! He is at all events man's Redeemer — his *mantle* is *dyed with blood* — and so he is the revelation of the very heart of God, his eternal *Word* of salvation embodied in human personality.

This rider and *his retinue* — the community of God's people as their clothing indicates (p. 125) — are assembling for the Battle of Armageddon to come in Scene 6. In the complementary scene of Act IV these were described as *the Lamb* and the *hundred, forty-four thousand martyrs,* their point of meeting being designated as Mount Zion.

This rider's *name* and the nature of the weapon he wields are of the greatest significance. This latter is *a sharp sword* proceeding *out of his mouth* (see 1:16; Eph. 6:4; Heb. 4:12). We have already noted that his opponents in waging war against him employ *three unclean spirits* which *spring* out of their *mouths* (p. 105)! The *sharp sword* of the *Word of God* is his answer to the foul badspel of the Dragon — it is the gospel content of the Church's evangelistic appeal. Armageddon, then, stands for that battle of ideologies which proceeds throughout the epoch of the Great Tribulation or the " last times." In that warfare the rider on the *white horse* will win, for he is " *Faithful" and " True"* — that is, the one destined to carry through the purpose of God to its final conclusion. Hence, the eventual title which is to be his — " *King of Kings and Lord of Lords.*"

## THE ANGEL STANDING IN THE SUN

Moreover, I beheld an angel standing in the sun!
He gave a shout in a mighty voice, crying to all birds flying in mid-heaven —

> "Come here. Gather to God's great feast.
>      Here you may eat
>              the flesh of kings,
>              the flesh of colonels,
>              the flesh of the mighty,
>              the flesh of horses and of those who ride them,
>              the flesh of everyone — of freemen and slaves,
>                      of small and great."

(19:17, 18)

God's great feast, indeed! In reality God spreads two banquets. One is designed for his own people — that of the marriage of his Son already mentioned in Scene 3 above. It had long ago been foretold by the Hebrew prophets, psalmists, and the incarnate Son himself (Isa. 49:9–12; 55:1 ff.; Ps. 23:5; Matt. 22:1 ff.). This is God's banquet of love — symbol of restored fellowship between himself and man.

The other feast that God spreads is the banquet of his wrath — it is this one that meets the eye on the field of Armageddon. And it is to this *feast* that the angel invites the *birds* of *midheaven*.

There can be no doubt that the scene here portrayed is taken from Ezek. 39:4, 17–20. There the Lord God is threatening destruction to " Gog, chief prince of Meshech and Tubal," who also appears below in this drama at Scene 7. God declares to this prince, according to Ezekiel, " I will give you to birds of prey of every sort and to the wild beasts to be devoured " (v.4). Then, he commands the prophet to assemble on the field of carnage the birds and beasts, employing words nearly identical to those of the angel in his summons here.

In numerous scenes hitherto we have had occasion to remark on the infinite mercy and forgiveness of God, who to the end would have men repent of their idolatries, fornications, sorceries, and murders and return to his obedience. Again and again throughout John's drama the refrain has arisen " But they would not! " Now, however, the end has come — no time remains in which man may repent of all his wickedness — and we may rest assured that they who die on the field of Armageddon do so only because to the last they have refused God's love. Small comfort this? Well, at all events, God's respect of men is such that he will force none to do his bidding.

## SCENE 6

## THE BATTLE OF ARMAGEDDON

Then I beheld the Beast and the kings of earth with their forces gathered together to do battle with Him who sat astride the horse and his followers.

Now, the Beast was captured and with it the false prophet who customarily performed miracles before it — miracles by reason of which those receiving the mark of the Beast and worshiping its image were led astray. Alive these two were then thrown into the lake of fire that burns with brimstone.

As for the rest — they were put to death by the sword proceeding out of the mouth of the Rider on the horse. So all the birds were gorged with their flesh. (19:19-21)

THE ACCOUNT of the Battle of Armageddon is sketched with a surprising lack of detail! Ever since the place name was given in Scene 6 of Act V, we have been anticipating a description of the terrain over which it would be fought and some account of the nature of the engagement. But even as far back as Scene 6 of Act III clear reference to a fierce fight between the forces of righteousness and wickedness was made. Further, certain features in that scene had led us to trace a distinct connection between this coming battle and the Great Tribulation of Scene 6, Act II. And there are still earlier references in Scenes 2 and 6 of Act I to the *hour of testing which is about to come upon mankind.*

The following series of equations, then, appears to be justified as representing John's thought — the Great Tribulation = the Battle of Armageddon = a war of ideologies (gospel versus badspel). The lack of detail, then, in the present scene ought not surprise us. For it is this battle which the seer has been all along describing throughout the drama — it is enough that here he should identify it as the great spiritual warfare that goes on throughout history between the worldly power (*the Beast*) and its *false prophet,* on the one hand, and the Rider on the *white horse* who wields *the sword proceeding out of* his *mouth* (the *Word of God*) and *his retinue,* on the other. Since, moreover, the Great Tribulation began with the incarnate life of our Lord and lasts through the entire history of the Church (p. 79), it is now clear that the Battle of Armageddon is an agelong struggle.

The destined result of this long warfare is that *the Beast* or secular power and its *false prophet* (the preachers of the badspel) are cast into the *lake of fire.* That is to say, they experience the *"second death"* (20:14) — banishment eternally from God's fellowship.

## Scene 7

## SATAN CAST INTO THE ABYSS

Again I beheld an angel descending from the sky and holding in his hand the key of the abyss together with a huge chain. He seized the Dragon, the ancient Serpent which is called by the names "Devil" and "Satan," and bound it for a thousand years. He cast it into the abyss, locked the same, and placed a seal upon it, that the Dragon might no more lead the nations astray — not until the thousand years are over. After that it is appointed that it shall be released for a short space of time. . . .

(20:1-3)

IN THE SCENE immediately preceding this, we witnessed the final end of *the Beast* and its *false prophet* — the secular power and the cultus that gave it a religious sanction. Now we are to witness the judgment of God on *the Dragon* that has all along been instigating rebellion against His rule among men.

Jewish and early Christian writers took quite seriously the Genesis account of creation in the space of " six days " and of God's final " rest " on the seventh (see Heb., chs. 3; 4). From Ps. 90:4 they concluded that one of creation's days was of a *thousand years'* duration (see II Peter 3:8 ff.). Hence, the " week of creation " — including the Sabbath of God's " rest " — was a matter of some seven thousand years. That God may rest during the seventh *thousand years,* it seems obvious that his enemy — the " *Devil,*" " *Satan* " — must be *bound* and so unable to make war against him. Accordingly, this fact is now stated before we are given in Act VII a picture of this epoch.

It would be quite wrong, of course, to imagine that John intends this *thousand years* to be taken literally any more than any other figure with which he deals in the drama. Whatever his contemporaries may have done, this prophet at all events employed the materials he found at hand to further spiritual ends and not for the solving of riddles of interest to the curious-minded. Accordingly, whereas the *thousand years* in question is one of " rest " for God, we shall see in the next act that it is not so for Christ and his Church!

The *Dragon* here and elsewhere is, of course, to be identified with *Apollyon* (p. 64), and so with the swarm of *locusts* which we have interpreted as the " corporate Sin " of the Race (p. 65). Accordingly, it is this Sin of mankind that is *bound* on earth because Christ is ruling in his Church during the millennium.

. . . So, when the thousand years are finished, Satan is to be loosed from his prison. He will come out again to deceive the nations that are at the four corners of the earth — both Gog and Magog — and to gather them together to battle. Their number will be, indeed, like the sand of the sea.

Well, they have gone up over the breadth of the earth — they have surrounded the camp of the saints and the Beloved City. But fire has come down from the sky and devoured them. So the Devil, their Deceiver, has been cast into the lake of fire and brimstone where are also the Beast and the false prophet. There shall they be tormented day and night forever and ever.

(20:7–10)

THIS PROPHECY of Satan's loosing and final end might as well be allowed to stand where it comes in John's book as here at the end of Act VI. As the verse numbers indicate (vs.7–10), it is inserted as a sort of parenthesis after the description of the stage setting for Act VII. We have placed it here, however, so as not to disrupt the continuity and so to destroy the overpowering effect of Act VII and its picture of the Church in the millennium.

No doubt John places it after the stage setting for Act VII, which follows immediately, because there we are to see the Church reigning with Christ and he wishes it to be clear that the forces of evil lie around *the camp of the saints and the Beloved City!* For we are not to take the suggestion too literally that the event described in this parenthesis happens *when the thousand years are finished,* nor that Satan's release is for *a short space of time.* We have already seen that such reference to time has various meanings with John (p. 57). We have also observed that John's literary method permits events to be recorded as in temporal sequence which are to be understood as simultaneous or even as simply different ways of saying the same thing (p. 81).

As we have already seen, John portrays Satan as endeavoring to duplicate God's rule at every point, including the life, work, death, resurrection, and return of the Messiah (p. 115). Here, therefore, we have the parousia or " second coming " of Satan and his hosts! But this is surely a mere literary device based on Ezek., chs. 38 and 39, as the allusions to *Gog* and *Magog* show. Here as there the denouement is swift, being accomplished by God's *fire* of judgment upon the final source of all evil. The clear intention of the passage is to say that with the millennial reign of Jesus Christ in his Church, God becomes " all in all." For Jesus " delivers the kingdom to God . . . after destroying every rule " that is not his (I Cor. 15:24).

# ACT
# VII

# VISION OF THE CHURCH IN THE MILLENNIUM

*Consummation of God's Purpose*
(Chs. 20:4–6; 20:11 to 22:5)

*Stage Setting:* The Church Enthroned with Christ (20:4–6)

THE FULFILLING OF GOD'S SEVENFOLD PLAN (20:11 to 22:5)

Scene 1   The Old Heaven and Old Earth Disappear (20:11)

Scene 2   The Last Judgment (20:12–15)

Scene 3   The New Heaven and New Earth (21:1)

Scene 4   The New Jerusalem (21:2–8)

Scene 5   Displaying and Measuring the New Jerusalem (21:9–21)

Scene 6   The City's Illumination (21:22–27)
          The Splendor of God and the Lamb

Scene 7   The City's Source of Life (22:1–5)
          The River and Tree of Life

*Stage Setting: The Church Enthroned with Christ* (20:4–6)

(In this act, we have essentially the same stage props as for Act II; that is to say, in the center appears the great white throne and on either hand the twenty-four seats arranged in a semicircle.)

*John, the Seer, concludes —*

Now, I beheld a number of thrones set out, that there were some who occupied them, and that judgment was committed to these latter. These were the persons who had been beheaded for their witness to Jesus, for the sake of the Word of God — they, indeed, who had not worshiped the Beast and its image nor accepted its mark on their forehead and hand. They had come alive and begun to reign with Christ a thousand years. The rest of the dead would not come alive till the thousand years were concluded. This reigning is the "first resurrection."

Blessed, then, is the saint who has a share in the "first resurrection" — over such the "second death" has no hold. Contrariwise, they shall be God's priests and the Messiah's people, and they shall reign with the latter for the thousand-year period. (20:4–6)

ND NOW, the millennium! — this is the epoch of the
Church's *reigning with Christ* for *a thousand years.* Persecuted and *beheaded for their witness to Jesus,* the community of
believers now sit on the twenty-four seats (*thrones*) which we
have observed arranged in *rainbow* fashion on either side of the
*great white throne,* where Jesus Christ himself for this epoch
sits enthroned (p. 43 and Luke 22:30). *Judgment* which is *committed* to them is a " Hebraism " or Jewish way of speaking of
the sovereignty which the Church exercises with its Lord in the
affairs of men (see the " Book of Judges," that is, of rulers).

As *God's priests* during this period, the Church achieves and
furthers the true worship of God. As *Messiah's people,* it serves
as Jesus' hands and feet, his eyes and ears and mouth in the
world. To employ Paul's expressive phrase, the Church is in the
world as the " Body of Christ," serving him as a man's body
does his every wish and purpose. Hence, the statement on p. 135
that, though the millennium brings " rest " for God, it does no
such thing for Christ and his Church! This is the period of
which Paul said of our Lord that " he must reign until he has
put all his enemies under his feet " (I Cor. 15:25) — thereafter
" he delivers the Kingdom to God the Father " (v.24).

This is, indeed, the epoch of the " *first resurrection,*" of the
new birth (John 3:1 ff.), of the ethical renewal (Rom. 6:1 ff.;
Eph. 2:1 ff.). It is in fact the epoch of the Church's entire life
on earth, of the Great Tribulation, or of Armageddon looked at
from a new standpoint — from that of the assured victory of
Christ's forces in the conflict with wickedness, rather than from
that of the hardships endured in achieving the same. The stage
setting here is, then, the same essentially as that for Act I —
only here stress is upon the Church's triumph rather than upon
its imperfections.

## THE OLD HEAVEN AND OLD EARTH DISAPPEAR

Again I beheld a great white throne and Him who occupied it.
From before his Presence earth and heaven fled away — no place, indeed, was found for them! (20:11) .

THE PLAY within the play! The action in Act VII all transpires in the presence of Jesus Christ and his Church whom we have just observed occupying the great white throne and the twenty-four seats which have been on stage ever since Act II.

The successive scenes of Act VII, then, are so many pageants representing the last things or events that occur at the end of history. To say that they all transpire before the thrones occupied by Jesus Christ and his Church is to say that the latter only have the spiritual insight to see them in their proper perspective! These possess such insight because as God's true servants they share his mind and can "think God's thoughts after him" (see I Cor. 2:9 ff.; 7:40). It may be said, then, that these scenes constitute the Church's understanding of the meaning of the eschatological events summarized in Act II, Scene 6, and which we have seen elaborated in succeeding acts.

Scene 1 brings onto the stage and before the reigning Church the first pageant — it presents us with the *great white throne* in duplicate, and before *him who occupies it, earth and heaven* are seen to be fleeing away! This is obviously a picture of God's judgment on his first creation and all pertaining thereto — the whole stands condemned in his eyes and in the eyes of Christ's Church which can now view all creation and history as he views them. This scene and the next together make up the deep shadows against whose background in succeeding scenes is to be thrown the brilliant light of God's everlasting Splendor. Judgment upon creation and history there must first be that there may be room for a new creation and a new history — those of God's eternal abode.

## THE LAST JUDGMENT

Moreover, I beheld the dead — the great and the small — standing before the throne. The books were opened — then, yet another book was opened — the Book of Life.

So the dead underwent judgment according to their works as these stood written on the books. The sea gave up its dead. Death and the grave surrendered up their dead. Then these were judged, each according to his works.

With that, death and the grave were flung into the lake of fire. This is the " second death " — that is to say, the lake of fire. If anyone was not found written up in the Book of Life, he also was flung into the lake of fire. (20:12–15)

A SECOND PAGEANT appears *before the throne* — it is the final *judgment* of all *the dead*. None are able to escape this august tribunal, whether they lie at the moment in *sea* or *grave*. *Death* releases its captives at God's express command.

Judgment here proceeds on two lines. There are, first, all *the books* in which a record of the *works* of the dead is recorded. Then there is also the *Book of Life*. The standard of judgment according to one's works is the usual one prescribed by the Scriptures from the earliest times (Ps. 62:12; Rom. 2:6). But the *Book of Life* in which the names of the blessed are *found written up* also has a long history behind it (see 3:5; Ps. 69:28; Luke 10:20).

The implication of the account — somewhat subtly expressed perhaps — is that man's works can never be of a character to satisfy God's absolute standard of judgment. For all whose names do not appear in the Book of Life — and the assumption must be that they are there by God's grace only! — are *flung into the lake of fire*. This latter symbolizes the "*second death*," or banishment along with *death and the grave* from God's Presence. All this is a symbolic way of presenting the same gospel as that found in such words as Paul's at Rom. 8:2; I Cor. 15:22, 45; and II Cor. 3:6, 17. First and last in this drama the one thing required for man's salvation is that faith on his part which suffers martyrdom because it has *declared God's Word and testified to Jesus* (1:9) — of such, as Jesus himself declared, he " will not be ashamed " (Mark 8:38), nor will he *ever blot his name out of the Book of Life* (see 3:5; Matt. 10:32).

That *death* is man's last enemy to be overcome by Christ is elsewhere taught by Paul (I Cor. 15:26, 55). It was also probably the view of the entire primitive Church (see Heb. 2:14 f.).

## THE NEW HEAVEN AND NEW EARTH

Then I beheld a new heaven and a new earth.

For the first heaven and the first earth had passed away, nor was the sea any more. (21:1)

THE THIRD PAGEANT to appear before the " mind's eye " of the spiritually discerning Church is the *new heaven* and *new earth*. " *Behold! I shall make all things new,*" declares God in Scene 4. He might well have remarked after this fashion in the present scene — for this is the new creation. The old creation was judged as unworthy because, as Paul remarks, God had " subjected " it " to futility " in view of man's sin (Gen. 3:17 ff.; Eccl. 1:2; Rom. 8:19 ff.). Creation, however, would " be set free from its bondage to decay and obtain the glorious liberty of the children of God," in Paul's thought and in that of many of his Jewish and Christian contemporaries. The day of that liberty has now come!

That the seven scenes of Act VII represent mere pageants passing rapidly before the eye of the reviewing Church and, so to speak, possessing no " solid substance " becomes quite clear when comparison is made of the contents of Scenes 1 through 3. For in Scene 1 the old heaven and old earth are seen passing away — dismissed by God's judgment upon them. And it is not until Scene 3 that a new heaven and new earth come into being. But in the meantime the judgment of all mankind is recorded in Scene 2! If, then, these scenes were to be taken as literally chronicling a succession of events and as possessing " solidarity," it should be obvious that in Scene 2 there would be nowhere for the judgment to proceed! But such a difficulty presents no problem when it is observed that in John's intention these scenes are viewed as so many pageants that are present to the mind of the millennial Church! To that mind Scenes 1 and 2 come together because both deal with the problem of judgment — the first relative to the old creation; the second, to mankind generally.

## THE NEW JERUSALEM

And now, I beheld the Holy City, New Jerusalem, descending out of heaven from God — readied like a bride when bedecked for her husband.

Moreover, I heard a loud voice declaring from out the throne —

> " Behold! God's dwelling is with men,
> He will dwell with them;
> They will be his people
> And he will be ' God with them.'
> He will wipe away every tear from their eyes.
> Death too will no longer be,
> Nor will there be any longer grief, clamor, distress.
> These former things have passed away."

Then the Occupant of the throne declared, " Behold! I shall make all things new."

And he added, " Write — for these words are faithful and true." Moreover, he said to me, " They are as good as accomplished — I am Alpha and Omega, the Beginning and the End. I shall freely grant to the thirsty to drink of the spring of the Water of Life. The Victor will inherit these things — I shall be God to him and he will be a son to me. But, to the cowardly and unbelievers, to blasphemers, murderers, fornicators, sorcerers, and idolaters, as well as to all liars, I shall assign their part in the lake that burns with fire and brimstone — such is the ' second death.' " (21:2–8)

I BEHELD A CITY! — from here to the end of the drama we are to have a series of pageants depicting in ever clearer detail the wonders of the *Holy City,* the *New Jerusalem.* John speaks, as always throughout this act, on behalf of the Church which is occupying " grandstand seats " as it proceeds. In Act I we saw the glorified Christ moving about among the *seven lampstands* of the historic Church as it was portrayed in quite realistic fashion. Here we are privileged to observe the same Church employing its moral and spiritual insight in viewing itself under the aspect of the *seven stars* — that is to say, as it appears in God's ultimate purpose and, as Paul would say, secure " in Christ " or, to employ John's own phrase, " in his right hand."

It will be recalled that *the Beast* was described under the form of *seven kings* and then of *an eighth by count* which was identified with the original seven, though having a sort of extra existence in his own right (p. 114). In this the Beast was merely mimicking the Church. For the historic Church is represented in Act I under seven aspects and now under an eighth as well — and this final aspect of the Church (its eternal character) has validity in its own right as representing God's ultimate will for it, though it would be a great mistake to suppose that the historic and eternal aspects of the Church are wholly to be separated in our thought.

The metaphor of God's *bride* as applied to God's people is an old one in prophetic thought (see Isa. 61:10; Hos., chs. 1 to 3; Eph. 5:26 ff.). That *God's dwelling is with men* is also a commonplace with the Hebrew prophets (Ex. 40:34; Isa. 7:14; Matt. 1:23). God is in the business of making men like unto himself in perfect holiness; in the appearance of *a son,* therefore, who bears his image his purpose in creation is complete!

## SCENE 5
# DISPLAYING AND MEASURING THE NEW JERUSALEM

Then there came to me one of the seven angels who hold the seven bowls that are full of the seven last plagues. He addressed me, saying: "Come here. I shall show you the bride, the wife of the Lamb."

So he carried me away in spirit to the top of a very high mountain. There he showed me the Holy City, Jerusalem, descending out of heaven from God. It shone with the Splendor of God — its brilliance was like that of a very precious stone — indeed, like a clear translucent crystal. It had a wall, massive and high, punctured by twelve gates. Twelve angels were embossed upon the gates and over them were inscribed the names of the twelve tribes of the sons of Israel. Three of the gates were toward the east, three toward the north, three toward the south, and three toward the west. The wall of the City had also twelve foundations upon which were engraved the twelve names of the twelve apostles of the Lamb.

Now, he who addressed me had a golden measuring rod with which to measure the City, its gates and its walls. The City lies foursquare, its length equal to its breadth. So, with the rod he found the City's dimensions to run to twelve thousand stadia in each direction, its length, breadth, and height being equal. Moreover, he found its wall's measure to be one hundred and forty-four cubits, according to the method of reckoning of a man, that is, of an angel.

The material of which the wall was made was translucent stone, while the City itself was of pure gold spun out like clear glass. The foundations of the City's wall were fashioned of every sort of precious stone — the first foundation was jasper, the second sapphire, the third chalcedony, the fourth emerald, the fifth sardonyx, the sixth sardis, the seventh chrysolite, the eighth beryl, the ninth topaz, the tenth chrysoprase, the eleventh hyacinth, the twelfth amethyst. Moreover, the twelve gates were twelve pearls — that is to say, each of the gates was made up of a single pearl. And the City's Broadway was of pure gold like transparent glass in appearance. (21:9-21)

THE SEER NOW BRINGS the *Holy City* nearer for our more careful inspection. It has not as yet been wholly realized on earth, as its *descending out of heaven from God* is intended to suggest — to see it in its entirety one must even yet be *carried away in spirit* to a *high mountain* from which proper perspective may be secured.

The description of this new *Jerusalem* is replete with suggestive phrases. As it is not only *the bride, the wife of the Lamb,* but also — as just indicated in Scene 4 — inhabited by those who have become victors and so God's sons, it shines *with the Splendor of God,* that is, with his holiness, truth, love, grace. The Greek word translated " splendor " (*doxa*) is the one employed in the Greek Old Testament wherever the Presence of God — in tabernacle and temple more particularly — is manifested by a luminous cloud, and it is intended to give expression to his perfection of ethical character (Ex. 29:43). God's purpose in making man was described from the first as intending that the latter should reflect this perfection as the moon reflects the light of the sun (Gen. 1:26 f.; Lev. 19:2). John's meaning, therefore, clearly is that this purpose of God is now fulfilled by the *Holy City* — the community of believers in Jesus Christ (see also II Cor. 3:16–18).

That the City is *measured* — as we have already seen — means that it is the object of God's saving activity (p. 71). This exhibits John's final purpose in writing the drama — everything in the old heaven and earth is adjudged as unworthy and so cast into *the lake of fire* (pp. 144, 148), save only the Church! Hence, the Church is now assured that the *twelve gates* of the City are wide enough and the *twelve foundations* of the same are strong enough to support all from *east, north, south,* and *west* who shall enter it to partake of the Kingdom banquet (Ezek. 48:31–35; Luke 13:29; Eph. 2:20; Heb. 11:10).

## THE CITY'S ILLUMINATION
### The Splendor of God and the Lamb

Now, I beheld no sanctuary in the City — for the Lord God Almighty is its sanctuary, as is also the Lamb. Nor has the City need of sun or moon to shine upon it — for the Splendor of God illumines it and its lamp is the Lamb. By its light will the peoples march forward; the kings of earth, moreover, will bring their splendor into it. Its gates will never be closed by day (there will be no night there to take into consideration); so they will bring the splendor and treasure of the nations into it. Nor will any unworthy thing nor he who does a contemptible or treacherous deed enter into it — on the contrary, only those who are written up in the Lamb's Book of Life. (21:22–27)

JOHN NOW BRINGS the *City* even closer than before that its interior may be the more readily studied by the observing Church. It now stands in the exact center of the stage! And yet, curiously enough, the seer's description of its most sacred spots is even more than is usual with him composed of selected verses from Scripture (see Isa. 60:1, 3, 5, 11, 19 f.)!

Two things stand out as we fix our gaze on this scene of eternal Splendor. In the first place, the *sanctuary* which has formed the background for this entire drama of the "last times" has at long last disappeared entirely! No shadow of it remains to obscure our unimpeded view of *God Almighty* and of the *Lamb standing — though it had the look of having been slaughtered —* before his Throne (p. 44). God himself and the Lamb have taken the sanctuary's place — it is their *Splendor* that *illumines* the Church's life — in the fullest sense imaginable God has become Emmanuel, God dwelling in the midst of his people!

The second point for which this scene is distinctive is the thought that *the peoples* and *kings of earth* bring into the New Jerusalem all their *splendor and treasure.* In other words, to the excellencies of the Church Universal all peoples have their distinctive contributions to make. They all *march forward* in the *light* of the Church, but equally they bring to it the gifts of character and life which God has given them to make. We are reminded by this scene of the words of the prophets — " It shall come to pass in the latter days that the . . . house of the Lord shall be established . . . and all the nations shall flow to it, and . . . walk in his paths " (Isa. 2:2–4; Micah 4:1–3).

## SCENE 7

# THE CITY'S SOURCE OF LIFE

### THE RIVER AND TREE OF LIFE

Then the angel showed me the River of Water of Life bright as crystal flowing out of the throne of God and the Lamb. Down the middle of the City's Broadway, as well as on either side of the River, the Tree of Life was planted. This Tree gives twelve kinds of fruit — each month seeing it produce a fruit which accords with the month. The Tree's leaves, moreover, have healing properties for the nations' ills; so that there will no longer exist a single " curse."

The throne of God and the Lamb will be in the City — there his servants will serve him — they will see his face and his name will be stamped on their foreheads.

Nor will there be any night there — they will have no need of light of lamp or light of sun, however, for the Lord God will shine upon them. Then, they will reign forever and ever. (22:1–5)

And now, the final scene of our drama! It takes us back in thought to the very beginning of God's creation of man. There the latter was placed in a " garden " — here he is transferred to a city, God being the " builder and maker " of both. In both appear a *River* and *the Tree of Life* (Gen. 2:9, 10). Man was driven forth from the Garden " lest he put forth his hand and take also of the tree of life, and eat, and live forever " (Gen. 3:22). But it was God's original design that man should " live forever " — provided man remain his loyal subject. Such loyalty is now assured and hence man is permitted free access to the City with its *River of Water of Life* and its *Tree of Life!* Much of this imagery comes from Ezek. 47:6 f., 12.

There is nothing new in paragraphs two and three opposite. But these serve as useful summaries of much that has already been said in this seventh act.

And so the curtain comes down finally upon this truly magnificent drama. Its closing note is that of Life — Life everlasting for God's people — Life lived in his Presence! Again, let us remind ourselves that the drama does not take us beyond the millennium — that is to say, beyond the long epoch of the Church's history from the manger in Bethlehem to the end of time and of history. But, as Act VII is intended to suggest, during this period the Church seated enthroned with Christ possesses the spiritual and moral insight to see into the " Beyond-History " and there to visualize that Life with God in eternity which is " life indeed "! It possesses this power because by faith the " Spirit of life in Christ Jesus " has already been at work in its historic existence (Rom. 8:2).

# EPILOGUE

*John, the Seer's, conclusion —*

The angel said to me: "These Words are trustworthy and true. The Lord God of the spirits of the prophets has sent his angel to show his servants the things that are appointed soon to occur." "Behold!" (says he) "I am coming speedily. Blessed is he who shall keep the Words of the prophecy in this Book."

It is I, John, who heard and beheld these things. And when I heard and beheld them, I fell down to worship at the feet of the angel who showed them to me.

But he said to me: "Look! Not that! I am your fellow servant — a compatriot merely of your brothers, the prophets, and of those who keep the Words of this Book. Worship God."

Then he added: "Do not seal up the Words of the prophecy in this Book. For the occasion appointed is near. Let the unrighteous keep on at his unrighteousness, the filthy in his filthiness; but equally let the righteous continue his righteousness, the holy his saintliness." "Behold!" (the voice of the Lord interjects) "I am coming speedily and my reward will be with me — to recompense each as his work merits. I am the Alpha and the Omega, the First and the Last, the Beginning and the End. Blessed are they who wash their stoles — it is their authority that will rest over the Tree of Life: it is they who will enter into the City by its gates. Without will be the dogs, sorcerers, fornicators, murderers, idolaters, and everyone who loves and fashions a lie." (22:6-15)

FOR THE SECOND TIME John remarks that he *fell down to worship at the feet of the angel* who was his guide and mentor (19:10)! In both cases it is in connection with his overpowering sense of the importance of the message contained in the *Words* which he hears — these are *God's verities* and so *trustworthy and true,* and the *witness concerning Jesus — prophecy,* indeed, at its richest (p. 127). In a very real sense they are to be identified with the rider on the *white horse* in Act VI, Scene 4, who is called *The Word of God* and who like them is described as "*Faithful*" *and* "*True*" — that is, as the fulfillment of God's ultimate saving purpose which it is the function of the gospel to proclaim (p. 129).

This is all very suggestive. It is John's way of giving in his epilogue a summary statement of the theme that he has been developing in his book. That theme is the gospel message or the Word of God set forth in the grand style of the Greek drama or of the Hebrew prophetic "rhapsody." Others among the New Testament writers presented that gospel in the simple narrative form known as "gospels" or in the didactic letter. John alone conceived the notion that the drama or rhapsody offered a novel literary model adapted to the gospel's presentation. In this form, therefore, he set forth his theology of history wherein Jesus Christ stands out as the central Personage on history's stage and his Church becomes the fulfillment of its final meaning and purpose.

John is no doubt conscious of using many of the artifices that were the "stock in trade" of contemporary writers of apocalypses. But he is far more vocal, at least, about his certainty that the content of his drama is *prophecy* in the best sense of the word and that it is as divinely inspired as were *the spirits of the prophets.*

## JESUS' IMPRIMATUR ON THE BOOK

"I, Jesus, have sent my angel to testify these things to you with reference to the churches. It is I who am the Root and Stock of David, the brilliant Morning Star."

## THE APPEAL OF THE SPIRIT AND CHURCH

The Spirit and the Bride say: "Come! Let him who hears also say, Come! And he who thirsts, let him come — he who desires, let him accept the Water of Life as a gift."

## JOHN, THE SEER's, TESTIMONY TO THE BOOK

I bear testimony to everyone hearing the Words of the prophecy in this Book that, if anyone adds to them, God will bring upon him the plagues written about in this Book; if anyone subtracts from the Words of the prophecy in this Book, God will "subtract" his part in the Tree of Life and in the Holy City, and in the things written about them in this Book.

The Witness to these things declares, "Yea! I am coming speedily."
*Amen! Come, Lord Jesus!*

(22:16–20)

NOTHING could be more fitting than that this gospel drama should be sent out under the imprimatur of Him who is both its central figure and hero — Jesus Christ! He it is whose *voice* was heard in Act I speaking to the narrator and who was seen on the cosmic stage dictating letters to his seven churches. Moreover, throughout the drama Jesus Christ in one or another character is represented as never far from the center of this stage. Now, therefore, as the real author, as well as principal actor of the drama, he signs his name and titles in token of the validity of its gospel message.

As for the actual proclaiming of the drama's gospel, this is the function of the *Spirit*-filled Church (the *Bride* of the Lamb). She issues her invitation, accordingly, quite fittingly in words taken from the evangelistic appeal in Isa. 55:1.

The seer himself follows this evangelistic appeal with a warning derived from Deut. 4:2 — where the reference is to the Law as God's revelation of his will to his people — and often repeated in the apocalyptic writings. Essentially this warning reflects the same sort of serious attitude toward the content of the gospel message as that exhibited by Paul in battling with those who would pervert and eventually destroy that message (Gal. 1:6–9). At the same time it gives evidence of John's expectation that his dramatic presentation of the gospel will have wide usefulness as an evangelistic agency in the historic Church (see also 1:3)!

The final *Witness* to the gospel is, however, Jesus Christ himself — the very Word of God — his is the final promise to come and fulfill this dramatic gospel on history's plane!

*Amen! Come, Lord Jesus!*